MW01449296

Productions in Print
Smith and Kraus Publishers, Inc.
177 Lyme Road, Hanover, NH 03755
www.SmithandKraus.com

Copyright © 2015 by David Ives. All rights reserved.

CAUTION: Professionals and amateurs are hereby warned that THE METROMANIACS is subject to a royalty. It is fully protected under the copyright laws of the United States of America and of all countries covered by the International Copyright Union (including the Dominion of Canada and the rest of the British Commonwealth), the Berne Convention, the Pan-American Copyright Convention, and the Universal Copyright Convention, as well as all countries with which the United States has reciprocal copyright relations. All rights, including professional, amateur stage rights, motion picture, recitation, lecturing, public reading, radio broadcasting, television, video or sound recording, all other forms of mechanical or electronic reproduction, such as CD-ROM, CD-I, information storage and retrieval systems and photocopying, and the rights of translation into foreign languages, are strictly reserved. Particular emphasis is laid upon the matter of readings, permission for which must be secured from the Author's agent in writing.

The English language stock and amateur stage performance rights in the United States, its territories, possessions and Canada for THE METROMANIACS are controlled exclusively by DRAMATISTS PLAY SERVICE, INC., 440 Park Avenue South, New York, NY 10016. No professional or nonprofessional performance of the Play may be given without obtaining in advance the written permission of DRAMATISTS PLAY SERVICE, INC., and paying the requisite fee. Inquiries concerning all other rights should be addressed to Abrams Artists Agency, 275 Seventh Avenue, 26th Floor, New York, NY 10001. Attn: Sarah Douglas.

ISBN-13: 978-1-57525-822-5

Cover Photo: Amelia Pedlow. Photo by Scott Suchman.
Cover Design: S. Christian Taylor-Low
Interior Layout: Elayna Speight
Editor: Heather C. Jackson
Manufactured in the United States of America

DAVID IVES

The Metromaniacs

Adapted from *La Métromanie* by Alexis Piron

Commissioned by:

SHAKESPEARE THEATRE COMPANY
Recipient of the 2012 Regional Theatre Tony Award®
Artistic Director Michael Kahn
Managing Director Chris Jennings

as part of its ReDiscovery Series.

The commissioning and world premiere production of *The Metromaniacs* was made possible by the generous support of The Beech Street Foundation

About the Shakespeare Theatre Company

Recipient of the 2012 Regional Theatre Tony Award®, the Shakespeare Theatre Company (STC) has become one of the nation's leading theatre companies. Today, STC is synonymous with artistic excellence and making classical theatre more accessible.

Under the leadership of Artistic Director Michael Kahn and Managing Director Chris Jennings, STC's innovative approach to Shakespeare and other classic playwrights has earned it the reputation as the nation's premier classical theatre company. By focusing on works with profound themes, complex characters and poetic language written by Shakespeare, his contemporaries and the playwrights he influenced, the Company's artistic mission is unique among theatre companies: to present theatre of scope and size in an imaginative, skillful and accessible American style that honors the playwrights' language and intentions while viewing their work through a 21st-century lens.

A leader in arts education, STC has a stable of initiatives that teach and excite learners of all ages, from school programs and acting classes to discussion series as well as accessible programs like the annual Free For All, one of STC's most beloved annual traditions, allowing audiences to experience Shakespeare at no charge.

Located in our nation's capital, STC performs in two theatres, the Lansburgh Theatre and Sidney Harman Hall in downtown Washington, D.C., creating a dynamic, cultural hub of activity that showcases STC as well as outstanding local performing arts groups and nationally renowned organizations. STC moved into the 451-seat Lansburgh Theatre in March 1992, after six years in residency in the Folger Library's Elizabethan theatre. At that time the Penn Quarter neighborhood was not considered desirable by many; since then, STC has helped drive its revitalization. The 774-seat Sidney Harman Hall opened in October 2007.

SHAKESPEARE THEATRE COMPANY

Administrative Offices
516 8th Street SE
Washington, DC 20003

202.547.1122
ShakespeareTheatre.org

About the ReDiscovery Series

During my first season as Artistic Director of the Shakespeare Theatre Company, we presented four plays. Three came from our namesake playwright, whose works from the basis of our theatre's repertoire. But for our fourth production, we chose Niccolo Machiavelli's 1518 play *The Mandrake* in an available translation.

Over the years the company has seen many changes, including expanding into two theatres in downtown Washington, D.C., to accommodate a growing audience for classic theatre. But even as our repertory has expanded to six or seven productions in a season, we continue to program only three plays by William Shakespeare. The rest come from the vast range of world dramatic writing including many important but little-known works. Our efforts to find and produce these works escalated in 1994 with the launch of the ReDiscovery Series, in which we investigate relevant and neglected plays of the classic canon through readings that are presented free of charge. After 15 seasons, many plays featured in the series have made their way onto our stages, including Musset's *Lorenzaccio*, Euripides' *Ion*, Lope de Vega's *The Dog in the Manger*, and Johnson's *The Silent Woman*.

We believe that to ensure that theses plays remain resonant and accessible to contemporary audiences, they need to be translated and adapted by the best modern writers. In our 2009-2010 Season, thanks to a grant from The Beech Street Foundation, we made our first commission: to David Ives to translate and adapt Pierre Corneille's comedy, *The Liar*. Less than two years later, we renewed our collaboration with David's new version of *The Heir Apparent* by Jean-François Regnard. We are pleased to be able to complete this trilogy of rediscovered French comedies with the addition of Alexis Piron's *The Metromaniacs*.

I have always believed that re-introducing these works to modern audiences and the American theatre community is an essential part of our mission in preserving and reinvigorating the classical repertoire. After their premieres on our stages, we hope these plays take their rightful place on stages throughout this country.

Michael Kahn
Artistic Director
Shakespeare Theatre Company

Metromania Mania
by David Ives

Frankly, I fell in love with the title.

Having enjoyed myself enormously adapting two French comedies of the 17th and 18th centuries for Michael Kahn and the Shakespeare Theatre Company, I was casting around for a third. In the course of reading in and about that period, I stumbled again and again upon mention of an obscure play from 1738 with a superb title: *La Métromanie*. It means, more or less, *The Poetry Craze*. ("Metro" from "metrum," Latin for poetic verse, and "mania" from... Oh, never mind.) As it happens, Drew Lichtenberg, STC's omniliterate literary manager, had noticed the title as well: potentially a real find for STC's wonderful ReDiscovery series, dedicated to bringing to light classic plays that had remained too long in undeserving darkness. It was via the ReDiscovery series that Michael and I had developed our two previous happy collaborations, *The Liar* and *The Heir Apparent*.

So I ordered the French text from the Internet and it arrived in a blurry offprint of an 1897 edition with an English introduction by a huffy scholar who heartily disapproved of the play and all its characters. Now I was interested. When I read that the play's author, one Alexis Piron, had failed to make the Académie Française because he'd written a lengthy poetic *Ode To The Penis*, I was really interested.

So what kind of play did the Bard Of The Hard-On write?

A very chaste and wonderfully delightful one. Upon inspection *La Métromanie* turned out to be a farce based on a brilliant idea, if given sometimes to long-winded declamations on Art. Its world is the airy, unmoored, Watteau-ish one that Piron's contemporary Marivaux would also put onstage. There's not much like realism in *The Metromaniacs*. We're in a levitated reality that's the exact counterpart of the vernacular, set-in-an-inn comedies the English were writing at the same time. This is champagne, not ale. Since it's about people who are mad for poetry, champagne is apropos, as is the fact that it's in verse. To dump this delicate play into prose would be to clip the wings of Pegasus and harness him to a plow.

The play was a lip-smacking scandal in its time, spinning into art what had been real-life comedy. It seems that all Paris had fallen in love with the poems of one Mademoiselle Malcrais de La Vigne, a mysterious poetess from distant Brittany (read: Appalachia). The celebrated satirist Voltaire publicly declared his love for the lady and her great works, only to have it revealed that Mlle de La Vigne was a guy named Paul Desforges-Maillard, very much living in Paris and taking his revenge on the poetry establishment for not appreciating his genius. Needless to say, Voltaire wasn't pleased when Piron's satire showed up (and showed him up). Worse than that, the show was a hit.

The premise was comic gold. The structural mechanics, I have to confess, turned out to be something else. Piron was a wit and a poet but not much of what I'd call a *farcifactor*, often content to let his characters intone his ravishing couplets without paying much attention to who just exited where or why anybody's doing anything. Besides those fatal disquisitions on Art, the play had not one but two male leads, a lackluster female ingénue and, like so many French plays of the period, it simply came to a stop rather than resolving. This is all by way of saying I've fiddled a good deal with Piron's masterpiece in bringing it into English. (The first English version ever, to my knowledge, but I'm open to correction).

When my friends ask me what it's about, I always say that *The Metromaniacs* is a comedy with five plots, none of them important. On the other hand, that's the beauty of the play, its purpose and part of the source of its delight. We go to certain plays to inhabit a world elsewhere, and *La Métromanie* is that kind of play in spades. Piron doesn't want plot. He wants gossamer and gorgeousness, he wants rarified air and helpless high-comic passion. A purer world. Characters drunk on language, fools in love with love. In other words, the way the world was meant to be.

Given what's in our newspapers day by day, a few yards of gossamer may be just what the doctor ordered. So gossam on, *mes amis*, gossam on…

About David Ives

David Ives has also adapted Molière's *Le misanthrope* (as *The School For Lies*), Corneille's *Le menteur* (as *The Liar*), and Regnard's *Le légataire universel* (as *The Heir Apparent*). He is the author of *All In The Timing*; *Venus In Fur* (both the play and the Roman Polanski film); *Time Flies*; *Lives Of The Saints*; *New Jerusalem*; and *Is He Dead?* (adapted from Mark Twain). He lives in New York City.

Lost Inside a Dream
by Drew Lichtenberg

The Metromaniacs opens on a special kind—a uniquely 18th-century kind—of scene. A well-to-do gentleman, one well-off enough to own an urban manse above the grime and grit of Paris, is putting on an amateur theatrical in his salon *des arts et des lettres*. The subject is *amour*, the play a dreamy device designed to reach his dreamy daughter. 100 suitors, a number drawn as if from Homeric myth, have gathered at the home in order to court her, but she is more interested in *Parnassus* (the literary magazine). The daughter, you see, prefers imagined romance to the real thing. So the father has fronted the money and written a play himself (*mais oui!*) to bring her back to reality. This may sound like a ludicrous if not downright fantastical scenario, but it is one that our author, Alexis Piron, bases upon close and accurate observation of Parisian literary life in the mid-1700s.

As Derek Connon points out, Voltaire's circle was fond of just such aesthetic larks. At the country house of his lover and patroness, Madame Du Châtelet, Voltaire frequently staged dramatic readings of his new plays. One reporter records, in 1734, the partial rehearsal and performance of 44 separate acts of plays and operas for an audience of aristocratic aesthetes—all within a 48-hour span. As *The Metromaniacs* testifies vividly, these events could often result in hilariously terrible art. Madame Du Châtelet may have translated Newton's *Principia Mathematica* into French, but according to one eyewitness, her attempts at acting were horrific enough to "induce vomiting."

There have always, it seems, been rich people convinced they were great artists, just as there have always been penniless poets in need of a patron. Our play's hero, Damis, is one such would-be genius. He has arrived with "two empty pockets and some ten-franc words," as his servant puts it, as well as a pseudonym befitting his ambitions and hiding his penury. He is one "Cosmo de Cosmos," just like the man born François-Marie Arouet, but known to the world as "de Voltaire."

Our milieu, in fact, *is* the Paris of the young Voltaire. This play—the talk of the town in 1738—was ripped from the headlines by Alexis Piron, a popular writer of low-brow potboilers and satiric farces. Piron seized on a literary scandal involving a poetry magazine, some cross-dressing in verse, and the red-faced Voltaire himself. It is a fragile and insulated ecosystem, this salon cosmos of the idle rich and their artistic hangers-on. Piron shows us characters at a remove from life. They build Edens on their parquet floors and escape into literary daydreams, living a life of fantasy. In short, their heads are stuck firmly up their aesthetic *derrieres*.

The France of the 1730s was one in which taxes on the middle-class had never been higher, nor their opportunities for social mobility more circumscribed. The royal coffers were bankrupt, depleted by the wars of the now-deceased "sun king," Louis XIV. His son, Louis XV, who took over the throne in 1715 at the age of five, was now well into his thirties, and still employing surrogates to rule in his ineffectual stead. Piron's own career reflects the changing times. Unwilling or unable to play the game of appeasing his patrons, he was exiled from the halls of *academe* and into the artistic (though financially profitable) purgatory of the unregulated fairground theatres. As an outsider to the artistic and political establishment, he was the ideal writer to provide a satirical portrait of a society in decadent decline.

But if *The Metromaniacs* is a social satire, it is a magnanimous one. This play is filled with memorable characters, all of them ultimately lovable, all of them redeemed by the engagement of their fertile imaginations with the sensual reality of their fellow human beings. Damis, intoxicated by ideas, meets his soul-mate in Francalou, flighty father and author of the amateur theatrical. If indolence is to be scorned, refulgence is to be celebrated. Within these woods, everyone can be who they really are by pretending, and theatrical transformation results in a strange kind of truth.

In other words, what begins as a social critique transfigures into the stuff of aesthetic daydreams, and vice versa. Piron mixes upstairs and downstairs, muddling the classes until he ultimately transcends them. The play's characters skirt the edge of optimistic allegory, and its cascade of ever-complicating plots overflows the theatre's tidy unities. Like Cervantes' *Don Quixote* or the *Gulliver's Travels* of Jonathan Swift, Piron's cross-channel contemporary, *The Metromaniacs* delights in a fantasy world commenting obliquely on its own society.

Did Voltaire, so embarrassed by this play, learn any lessons from it? Could it have been swirling in the ether when he wrote his own allegorical-satirical-fantastical masterpiece, *Candide*, over two decades later, in 1759? We'll never know. Courtesy of David Ives, let's give the last word to our *ami*, Damis:

> Unlike those chatterers who speak in herds,
> We speak the best of all possible...words.

About Alexis Piron

One of the most widely produced comic writers of the 18th century, Alexis Piron (1689-1773) lived a life dogged by controversy and topicality, rivalry and ribaldry. Indeed, Piron, who once said that he "farted epigrams," was as well known for his personal feuds as his satirical writings. His ability to make powerful enemies, combined with his Falstaffian zest for the low life, helps to explain his contemporary obscurity. For every creative triumph that flagrantly flouted the rules, Piron seemed to run into direct conflict with the Parisian cultural establishment. The life of the party in his own times, he is all but forgotten today.

Born in 1689 in Burgundy, Piron showed an early knack for poetry and knavery. Witness his "Ode to the Penis," an enthusiastic epistle addressed to his member, written when he was still a teenager. Though his father wanted him to study law, he moved to Paris to write for the stage, shortly after the death of Louis XIV in 1715.

Instead of writing, however, for the Comédie Française—the officially sanctioned theatre of the French ruling classes—Piron made his debut at the unofficial fairground theatres located outside the city. At these *théâtres de la foire*, Parisians came to have a naughty good time, classical decorum be damned. They were periodically closed down by the Comédie Française, which eventually obtained a bizarre legal injunction that forbid fairground authors from employing more than one speaking character.

In *Arlequin Deucalion* (1722), Piron solved this restriction ingeniously. Harlequin, the lone survivor of a biblical flood, entertains himself by acting out scenes from the underwater Comédie Française, sprinkling in satirical jabs at 18th-century plays, actors and authors. Part sketch comedy, part literary ventriloquism, part enraging satire, the play established Piron as an unofficial enemy of "high art" and an anarchic, dangerous wit.

Over the next decade, Piron would move confidently from one mongrel, "low-brow" genre to another. In 1738, however, Piron produced his unexpected masterpiece, at, of all places, the Comédie Française. Inspired by a real-life literary scandal involving Voltaire, *La Métromanie* satirizes the literary pretensions of the ruling classes, bringing poetic delusions of honor and glory down to the parterre of public opinion. "What is this *Métromanie* by that maniac Piron!" Voltaire wrote a friend when hearing about the play. "I fear this will not be pleasant." The play was a popular success, and one that Voltaire would not forget.

In 1753, Piron was nominated to the famed Académie Française (of which Voltaire was a member). Louis XV vetoed him, citing the impropriety of his adolescent *Ode a Priape,* though many believe the reasons were more personally motivated. Though he lived a long life of material comfort, Piron was never produced again at the Comédie Française. For his epitaph in 1773,

Piron wrote his final, and most famous, couplet:
> Ci-gît Piron, qui ne fut rien
> Pas même académicien.

As David Ives translates it:
> Here lies Piron, a nothing, an anatomy.
> He couldn't even make the French Academy.

Piron's Plays

1689	Alexis Piron is born in Dijon, Burgundy, in a region famous for its mustard (*dijonaisse*), wine (*burgundy, mais oui*), and beef (*bourgignon*).
c. 1708-9	Piron – "Ode to the Penis" (*Ode à Priape*). Piron narrowly avoids calls to prosecute him for obscenity.
1713	The War of the Spanish Succession ends, Louis XIV's unsuccessful attempt to place his grandson on the Spanish throne.
1715	Upon the death of King Louis XIV, Louis XV becomes king at age five.
1718	The Comedie Francaise obtains a legal judgment limiting the spectacles at the fairground theatres (*theatres de la foire*) to one speaking part. This absurd legislation strengthens the Comedie Franciase's monopoly and threatens to ruin the unregulated theatres outside the city limits.
1719	At the age of 30, after failing the bar exam, Piron moves to Paris. He works as a copyist for the Chevalier de Belle-Isle (grandson of Nicholas Fouquet, Louis XIV's superintendent of finances). He is paid meagerly.
1722	Piron makes his theatrical debut in the fairgrounds with *Arlequin Deucalion*. The piece is an enormous success, obeying the one speaking-character law while constantly threatening to transgress it.
1722-32	Either solo or with Alain-Rene Lesage (author of *Turcaret*), Piron pens 21 more pieces at the *theatres de la foire*, many of them parodies of tragedy or grand opera.
c. 1723	At the house of the Marquise de Mimeur, Piron meets Voltaire. They take an immediate dislike to one another. Piron takes a liking, however, to the Marquise's servant, whom he marries in 1741.
1726	Jonathan Swift – *Gulliver's Travels*
1728	John Gay – *The Beggar's Opera*
1729	*The Mercure de France* affair. Voltaire is humiliated after writing a love poem (in the *Mercure*, a literary magazine) to a female poetess from Brittany who turns out to be a man in Paris.
1730	Marivaux – *The Game of Love and Chance*
1738	Piron – *La Métromanie*. The play, inspired by the *Mercure de*

	France affair, is a great success, though it would not be revived until ten years later.
1743	Goldoni – *The Servant of Two Masters* in Venice.
1744	Louis XV bans all *opéras comiques* at Parisian fairground theatres, as part of the continuing attempt to preserve the Comedie Francaise's monopoly.
1751	The first *Encyclopédie* is published, featuring contributions from Diderot, Voltaire, Rousseau, and d'Alembert.
1753	Piron is nominated for membership to the Academie Francaise, but Louis XV vetoes his candidacy, citing his youthful writings (See 1708). Piron's partisans obtain a pension from him equal to the pension for an "academician."
1759	Voltaire - *Candide*
1762	Mozart tours Europe as a six-year-old prodigy. He stays in Paris with the German-born critic Baron Grimm, who once called Piron an "epigrammatic machine."
1763	The Seven Years' War ends, marking the end of France's reign as a major European power and the rise of Prussia.
	In the war's North American theater, known as the French and Indian War, France and Spain lose their North American colonies to Britain.
1769	Lessing – *The Hamburg Dramaturgy*
1773	Piron dies.
	The Boston Tea Party
1774	Louis XV dies, leaving the French monarchy at its political, financial, and moral nadir

DAVID IVES

The Metromaniacs

Adapted from *La Métromanie* by Alexis Piron

Commissioned by:

S **SHAKESPEARE THEATRE COMPANY**
Recipient of the 2012 Regional Theatre Tony Award®
Artistic Director Michael Kahn
Managing Director Chris Jennings

as part of its ReDiscovery Series.

The commissioning and world premiere production of *The Metromaniacs* was made possible by the generous support of The Beech Street Foundation

Please note: this is a pre-production version of the script.

This adaptation of *The Metromaniacs* was first performed by the Shakespeare Theatre Company at the Lansburgh theatre in Washington, D.C., where it opened on February 9, 2015, under the direction of Michael Kahn.

Original cast
(in order of speaking)

FRANCALOU
Adam LeFevre*

LISETTE
Dina Thomas*

MONDOR
Michael Goldstrom*

DAMIS
Christian Conn*

DORANTE
Tony Roach*

LUCILLE
Amelia Pedlow*

BALIVEAU
Peter Kybart*

* Member of Actors' Equity Association,
the Union of Professional Actors and Stage Managers.

Original production team:

Director
Michael Kahn

Set Designer
James Noone

Costume Designer
Murell Horton

Lighting Designer
Mark McCullough

Sound Designer
Matt Tierney

Composer
Adam Wernick

Period Movement Consultant
Frank Ventura

Voice and Dialect Coach
Ellen O'Brien

Casting Director
Laura Stanczyk, CSA

Resident Casting Director
Carter C. Wooddell

Literary Manager/Dramaturg
Drew Lichtenberg

Assistant Director
Craig Baldwin

Production Stage Manager
Bret Torbeck*

Assistant Stage Manager
Elizabeth Clewley*

* Member of Actors' Equity Association,
the Union of Professional Actors and Stage Managers

The Metromaniacs Characters

Metromaniac. Noun. A person addicted to poetry, or to writing verses. (From Latin metrum, poetic meter + Greek mania, madness.)

DAMIS, a young poet

DORANTE, a young man in love with Lucille

LUCILLE, a young woman in love with poetry

LISETTE, Lucille's maid

MONDOR, Damis's valet

FRANCALOU, Lucille's father

BALIVEAU, Damis's uncle

The setting is the ballroom of Francalou's house in Paris. Spring, 1738.

FRANCALOU	*Fraynk*-a-loo
LISETTE	Lee-*zett*
MONDOR	Mahn-*dorr*
DAMIS	Dah-*mee*
DORANTE	Dor-*ahnt*
BALIVEAU	*Bal*-a-voe
MERIADEC	*Mair*-ya-deck
PEAUDUNCQVILLE	Po-dunk-*veel*
BOUILLABAISSE	*Bool*-yuh-bezz
COMEDIE	Ko-may-dee
FRANCAISE	Frahn-sezz
MELPOMENE	Mel-*pom*-a-nee
ST. SULPICE	Sann-syool-*peece*
STUMM	Shtoom (keep it quiet)

Note: Parenthesized dialogue indicates an aside to the audience.

For scansion, the words "poet" and "poem" sometimes count as two syllables, sometimes one depending on the verse. Ditto "didn't," "isn't," and "even." "Poetry" is sometimes two syllables, sometimes three.

Once again, for Michael Kahn:
The Metromaniacs' perfect host.
— *David Ives*

ACT ONE

(Spring, 1738. The ballroom of Francalou's house in Paris, most of it concealed right now by a show curtain. FRANCALOU and LISETTE ENTER through the audience.)

FRANCALOU
(trumpeting as he enters; then:)
A fanfare! Good! To spark the celebrations.

LISETTE
It's touch and go. There could be complications.

FRANCALOU
But what about our *show*? The stage is set?
The actors and musicians, they've all met?

LISETTE
Yes, sir.

FRANCALOU
All right, then. Curtain up, Lisette!

LISETTE
You said you wanted something magical...

(LISETTE opens the curtain, revealing a "wood" of painted trees and a couple of "rocks." A full "moon" hangs over it all.)

FRANCALOU
I love it! *Yes*! What's more theatrical
Than this: an artificial sylvan wood
Where yesterday my Paris ballroom stood?
These trees, this Eden sprouting from parquet—
A perfect setting for my humble play!

LISETTE
You've got some dappled shade, bright-fading moon.

FRANCALOU
It just wants fawns with pan-pipes playing a tune.
My guests, now, and my daughter, they'll go where?

LISETTE
I thought we'd put the audience out there. [*Points to audience.*]

FRANCALOU
Brilliant! They'll stroll in here, digest, relax—
And we'll serve up *The Metromaniacs*!
Of course, I only wrote it for a laugh.

But here and there 's a joke, a paragraph,
A rhyme or two I might not call un-juicy.
What a choice welcome-home gift for my Lucy!

LISETTE
She won't be shocked to see herself portrayed?
And played by me, monsieur?

FRANCALOU
Well, you're her maid!
Who else could send her up with such finesse?

LISETTE
You know she likes to wear that rosy dress?
I forged a copy that will make us *blur*.
In costume, sir, I swear you'll think I'm her.

FRANCALOU
You'll do her languid slouch, the drawl, the twirl?

LISETTE
(twirling a lock of hair)
You mean *Whatever, Dad...*"?

FRANCALOU
Yes! That's my girl!
With luck, by seeing herself she'll come alive,
Re-find her natural energy, revive!

LISETTE
Maybe if Lucy didn't read all day...

FRANCALOU
The remedy's right here! This very play!
My comedy will cure her foul ennui,
Make her the hurricane she used to be!
What's all her indolence but ignorance
That life's for laughing and that we're its jests?
Maybe she'll find a mate amongst my guests.
A hundred men might warm her virgin winter.

LISETTE
You might find someone.

FRANCALOU
I?

LISETTE
A willing printer.
For, sir, with all the poems and plays you write—
You scribble all day long and half the night!

FRANCALOU
The Muses have bestowed on me an itch.

LISETTE
If you could just get published...

FRANCALOU
Oh, that's rich!
HA, HA, HA, HA!

LISETTE
Monsieur? Hello? Do I detect some glee?

FRANCALOU
Yes, but the laugh's on this, Lisette, [*shows MAGAZINE*] not me.
Parnassus, our top literary rag.
I send them poems and they do what? They *gag*.

LISETTE
Didn't they call you...?

FRANCALOU
"A rhyming ignoramus."
What they and you don't know—is that I'm famous!
Now keep this mum. No idle scuttlebutt.

LISETTE
Monsieur, these two lips are epoxied shut.

FRANCALOU
Justice! Oh, my revenge has been so sweet!
Each week, *Parnassus* runs a lyric tweet
From a strange poetess in distant Brittany.
She's caused a firestorm with her far-out poetry.
A "genius," all our biggest brains concur.
Well, how's this for a laugh? Lisette, *I'm her*.

LISETTE
This woman?

FRANCALOU
With a pen-name that's ideal.
I write as "Meriadec de Peauduncqville"!
And it's all garbage! Tripe! Is it not sad
Some Breton cretin could become a fad?
My greatest fan's *Damis*, a poet-fool
Who every issue bathes himself in drool.
And *this* week, oh, Lisette, you're going to crow,
Damis asks for my hand in marriage.

LISETTE
No!

FRANCALOU
(reads from Parnassus*)*
"Mad Shepherdess, you have ewes, I have rams,
Should we not couple flocks—and epigrams?
Wed me and lo! how high my heart has leapt!"
So what do you think, Lisette? Should I accept?

LISETTE
That's up to you. Or, *ewes*. But while we're blathering
The party's started and your guests are gathering.

FRANCALOU
Yes, yes, and I've a million things to do.

(MONDOR ENTERS.)

MONDOR
Excuse me, sir, is your name Francalou?

FRANCALOU
Just ask Lisette, she'll help you. Toodle-oo!

(FRANCALOU EXITS.)

MONDOR
"Lisette," is it? And you're his aide-de-camp?

LISETTE
You are…?

MONDOR
Mondor! Valet and gifted scamp!
Among my talents being a knack for kissing.

LISETTE
And you're here why?

MONDOR
My master has gone missing.
He should be here, according to my dope.

LISETTE
Your boss's name?

MONDOR
Damis. You know him?

The Metromaniacs

LISETTE
                                    Nope.
But wait. "*Damis*"...that somehow rings a bell...

MONDOR
And then there's always me.

LISETTE
             Nice try.

MONDOR
                                    Ah, well.
(*LISETTE starts out. HE heads her off.*)
But hey, before we wave and say ciaobella,
Consider this: am I a lucky fella?
To find myself here in this ritzy house
With you, a maid who's made to be my spouse?

LISETTE
A maid who's made for richer men than you. [*Starts out again.*]

MONDOR
This *is* the home of Monsieur Francalou...?

LISETTE
It is.

MONDOR
    He's got an only child?

LISETTE
            That's right.

MONDOR
She just got home from college?

LISETTE
                           Late last night.

MONDOR
You're putting on some kinda play, or show?

LISETTE
A set, a moon, some painted trees. Hel-LO!

MONDOR
There's fireworks? Dinner? Dancing? All that jazz?
Plus bachelors, to add to the pizzazz?

LISETTE
A hundred suitors, each one hot to be here.

MONDOR
This is the place! My master's *got* to be here!

LISETTE
Okay. His looks? His hair? His build? His cloak?

MONDOR
Oh, you can't paint Damis in just one stroke.
Depending on his mood or what he's thinkin'
His looks'll change without him even blinkin'.
I swear! He's thin one minute, now he's squat,
He's blue-eyed, now he's brown-eyed, now he's not.
He works all day but never does a thing.
He'll pace, he'll moan, stand on one leg, he'll sing.
Most of the day he spends inside his mind—
His head stuck firmly up his own behind.

LISETTE
So he's a poet.

MONDOR
Right! You know these nerds!
Two empty pockets and some ten-franc words!

LISETTE
We have a poet-guest.

MONDOR
It's him! Or he.

LISETTE
The problem is, his name is not Damis.

MONDOR
Well, lead me to him. Then we two can play.

LISETTE
He's coming now—so you boys play away.

(LISETTE EXITS. DAMIS ENTERS, writing in a NOTEBOOK.)

MONDOR
Monsieur...

DAMIS
Mad Shepherdess, can it be you?
O, bliss! It's you, who like celestial dew

The Metromaniacs

Silver each daisy through your argent art!
As it is you who own my ardent heart!

MONDOR
Yeah, look...

DAMIS
Ye GODS, must we two live in twain?
Who are one heart, one soul, a single bwain? Brain?
Come tend my flocks with me forevermore!
Marry me!

MONDOR
Sir...

DAMIS
What is it now, Mondor?
How long have you been there? Aren't you embarrassed?

MONDOR
Look, I been chasing you all over Paris!
Nobody knows you here, what is this game?

DAMIS
Well, did you ask for me *by my own name*?

MONDOR
How else? Aren't you my boss, Monsieur Damis?

DAMIS
Shut up! Or you'll alert some buzzing bee.
Within these walls I've got a *nom de plume*.

MONDOR
A different name? It's oddball, I assume.

DAMIS
"Cosmo de Cosmos"!

MONDOR
Perfect! Oh, that's *ace!*
Cosmos! A synonym for *empty space*.

DAMIS
That name's a passport pungent as chartreuse.

MONDOR
Yeah, getting back to *earth?* I've got bad news...
[Produces some BILLS.]

DAMIS
It won me entry to this fecund house
Whose owner treats me like some second spouse.

MONDOR
Monsieur...

DAMIS
Why not? The way I dazzle him!
At meals, extempore, I frazzle him,
Shoot coruscating phrases toward the skies
So luminous he has to shield his eyes!

MONDOR
...I've got...

DAMIS
Poor fool, he thinks he too can write.
But God, his stuff's so limp, so lame, so trite.

MONDOR
...BAD NEWS.

DAMIS
Oh, will you cease your litany?
We're leaving.

MONDOR
Leaving? *This*?

DAMIS
For Brittany.

MONDOR
Brittany? That's nowheresville, it's outer sticks!
The chicks there carry Brittany spears! They're hicks!

DAMIS
It's where I'll meet my predetermined dove.
You see, my trusty servant, I'm in love.

MONDOR
Who, you?

DAMIS
Yes, me.

MONDOR
With who?

The Metromaniacs

DAMIS
With *whom*.

MONDOR
Who's she?

DAMIS
My natural partner! A celestial bard
Whose poems have rocked the Paris avant-garde!

MONDOR
And this broad, *bard*, has a name? A name that's real?

DAMIS
Her name is Meriadec de Peauduncqville!
That's where she lives.

MONDOR
In Peauduncq...?

DAMIS
Peauduncqville.

MONDOR
When did this happen? Why'd I never glean her?

DAMIS
How could you know of her? I've never seen her.

MONDOR
WHAT?!

DAMIS
No one has—except through reading glasses
By gazing on her poems here in *Parnassus*. [*Shows MAGAZINE.*]
Works of sheer genius from a coarse Bretonne!
Can't you see her, in cap and rough cretonne,
Scribbling a poem while milking some sad goat?
Producing masterworks beside a stoat?
Hermited all alone up there...aloof...

MONDOR
Master, you are a master.

DAMIS
Rhymester?

MONDOR
Goof.
You see these bills? You're broke, with zip to borrow!

DAMIS
Mondor, I'm going to pay all those *tomorrow!*

MONDOR
Oh. Great. I mean, if what you say is true...

DAMIS
So what's the damage? To the final sou. My tailor?

MONDOR
Fifty.

DAMIS
Barber?

MONDOR
Hundred twenty.

DAMIS
Landlord?

MONDOR
Two C-notes.

DAMIS
Grocer?

MONDOR
Oh, sir, plenty. Plus all my wages.

DAMIS
Dating from?

MONDOR
The Middle Ages.

DAMIS
I have the money.

MONDOR
In your hand? Who says?

DAMIS
(produces a THEATRE BILL)
This flyer from the Comédie Française.

MONDOR
"The Talking Flute." Monsieur, what is this crap?

DAMIS
A comedy that's bound to cause a flap.
Debuting tonight, composed by whom but me.

MONDOR
It says "*By Bouillabaisse.*"

DAMIS
My stage name. See?
I'm all the rage before the curtain falls,
You get your wages at the curtain calls.

MONDOR
I'm gone. [*Starts out, DAMIS pulls him back.*]

DAMIS
Mondor, this vehicle's pure pork!
It'll tour everywhere! Marseilles, New York.
Then, riding on my name…

MONDOR
Which name?

DAMIS
My name,
I marry Meriadec at Notre Dame.

MONDOR
Dom.

DAMIS
Dame. We breed some kids with acme wits
Who still with acne start producing hits!
Our first a new Molière, a comic master,
Our second a Racine who does disaster,
A third who in the opera writes a smash,
Our novelist daughter's raking in the cash,
And you'd leave me when we're this, no, *this* close?
With points not on the net but on the gross?

MONDOR
You haven't even *met* this dame! You're crazy!

DAMIS
I grant you, some of the details are hazy.

MONDOR
Yeah, what if she's a dog? She send a photo?

DAMIS
Great poetesses don't look like Quasimodo.
Pack up. [*Starts out, MONDOR pulls him back.*]

MONDOR
But I just met this maid, real kitteny…

DAMIS
Good. You can write, inviting her to Brittany. [*Starts out.*]

MONDOR
But…but… She's *here!*

DAMIS
Who's here?

MONDOR
Your Meria-broad.

DAMIS
You mean under this roof?

MONDOR
I swear to God! [*Winks to audience.*]

DAMIS
She's in this house? Where is she?

MONDOR
In…cognito.

DAMIS
My God, I sense the stirrings of libido!

MONDOR
Already? That's what I would call rapport!

DAMIS
I am poet to the bone, Mondor!
My stock in trade is actualizing dreams.
Poets love love! We're sated by what seems!
Then, unlike chatterers who speak in herds,
We seek the best of all possible…words.
I'm going to find her! Press her to my side!

(DAMIS EXITS.)

MONDOR
(calls after him)
But sir, there's *more* bad news! [*To us:*] Okay, I lied.

She isn't really here, his phantom bride.
But hey, all's fair in love and comedy.
(LISETTE ENTERS.)

LISETTE
Are you still here?

MONDOR
Divine Melpomene!

LISETTE
(from twenty feet away)
Slap!

MONDOR
Ow! You coulda settled for a shrug.

(DORANTE ENTERS.)

DORANTE
Lisette?

LISETTE
Monsieur Dorante?

DORANTE
Give us a hug!

MONDOR
Have I a rival, madam? Who's this bug?
All right, then, fine. I'll go, if that will please you!

(MONDOR EXITS.)

LISETTE
Sir, how did you get in? What if he sees you?

DORANTE
Who, Francalou? He's never seen my face.
So, wow! He keeps a forest in his place…?

LISETTE
Francalou is your father's bitterest foe.

DORANTE
That ancient libel suit of theirs, I know.
But what's to me their years of legal slaughter?
And aren't you throwing a party for his daughter?
The fair Lucille, our city's brightest match,
A plum whom some fine bachelor should catch?

LISETTE
Oh, sir. Not *her*. You're mad! It's bonafide!

DORANTE
Where is she? Lead me to my future bride!

LISETTE
Lucille?

DORANTE
I idolize the girl, Lisette.

LISETTE
One small detail? *You two have never met.*
You'd settle for a sight-unseen romance?

DORANTE
Lisette, are you forgetting? This is France!
I hear she's handsome. And she's well-to-do.

LISETTE
She's worth a million francs.

DORANTE
                     Well, I'm worth two.

LISETTE
Her Dad has asked a hundred men here, son!

DORANTE
Then count me in. I'll make a hundred one.

LISETTE
But if...

DORANTE
Enough what-ifs! Aren't I a steal?

LISETTE
Monsieur Dorante, this is the limp Lucille!
A prize? Oh, yeah. These hundred guys are proof.
But sir, she's pathologically *aloof*.
She's distant, she's inert, she's nonchalant.
She sure would never flirt with some Dorante.
I'd be amazed if she were ever wived,
Locked in her room *reading* since she arrived.
See, she's a metromaniac. That's her curse.

DORANTE
Crazy for subways?

LISETTE
No, crazy for verse.
And inflammation of the mental bursa
Where verse becomes your vice, and vice-a-versa.

DORANTE
Poetry, huh.

LISETTE
Especially poems with sheep.
A shepherd with a harp? She thinks that's deep.
She's scribbling poems up there all night and day.
And you would take Lucille to wife? Oy vey!

DORANTE
It's not a natural match, when you consider it.

LISETTE
She's an anthology and you're illiterate!
But here comes Venus, rising from the ink.
Shoo!

(DORANTE hides in "the woods" as LUCILLE ENTERS. She wears a sky-blue dress and twirls a lock of her hair.)

LUCILLE
Morning, Lizzie.

LISETTE
Afternoon, I think.

LUCILLE
Whatever...Listen, what's this crowd about?

LISETTE
Thinking you something to be proud about,
Your father's throwing you a great big party.

LUCILLE
Oh. Cool...

LISETTE
A hundred men, each hale and hearty.
These males don't make you slightly lose your poise?

LUCILLE
Boys are all right, I guess—if you like noise.
(Wandering in the "trees," oblivious of them. DORANTE hides.)
In this loud world one wants a quiet glade,

A sylvan forest where there's dappled shade,
A rock or two, a moon that's always bright...
Is this a forest?

LISETTE
                For our play tonight,
This glade's the inside of a co-ed's brain
Who too much poetry has driven insane.

LUCILLE
Wow. I could swear I know a girl like her!
No, really. Can't you see this character?
A heroine who's mad for the Ideal,
Who scorns the sordid, sweaty, petty Real,
Where all is buyable and biddable.
She wants The Undoable, Undiddable,
A world of people eloquent and deep
Where shiny men tend perfect little sheep.
She's probably a rich girl, slightly sad,
Who's had it all and, driven slightly mad,
Wanders a mansion looking rather scruff,
Petting a small stuffed toy, her weasel, Fluff.

(She produces, briefly, a small STUFFED TOY.)

LISETTE
Looks like our play is true to life enough.
Nice chance for you to meet the bachelor classes.

LUCILLE
I'd rather read this issue of *Parnassus*. [*Shows the MAGAZINE.*]
Commune with *Him*.

LISETTE
                A guy? Who is this "he"?

LUCILLE
My shepherd minstrel?

LISETTE
                Yeah.

LUCILLE
                His name's *Damis*.
God keep his flocks and bless his warbling notes.
I see him now, scribbling amidst his goats.

LISETTE
Wait. Someone said he's *here*! I swear to God!

LUCILLE
My hero? Wielder of Apollo's rod?

LISETTE
Yeah, him! A real Olympian torpedo!

LUCILLE
Where is he? Tell me, Liz!

LISETTE
He's in...cognito.
So circulate!

LUCILLE
I'll meet him?

LISETTE
You can try.
Or if not him, why not some other guy?
Like one who doesn't want to push a plow.

LUCILLE
My hair's a mess. Mwah! Thank you, Lizzie. Ciao!

(LUCILLE EXITS. DORANTE ENTERS from "the wood.")

LISETTE
See what I mean? Monsieur? Monsieur...you heard?

DORANTE
I saw a vision! Didn't hear a word.

LISETTE
What's this? What are you doing on your knees?

DORANTE
It's love! Oh, help me win her, Lizzie, please!

LISETTE
You want to guide *her* toward a marriage bed?
You'd have to pry her first from her own *head!*

DORANTE
I'll do it! Anything! Just name the task!
Does she want wine? I'll find the finest cask!
Tulips, like her two lips? I'll grow a tree!

LISETTE
A tree won't work.

DORANTE
What would work?

LISETTE
Poetry.

So write some!

DORANTE
Me?

LISETTE
The perfect calling card!
An Ode To Livestock? Baby, she'll fall hard.
Cough up a canto, or a triple distich.

DORANTE
I don't know what those are. I'm not artistic!

LISETTE
A double dactyl? Something to enchant...

DORANTE
I'd talk in rhyming couplets, but I can't!
She doesn't just lack some necessary enzymes?

LISETTE
What Lucy lacks are necessary end-rhymes.
Without some verses you will never get her
And she will never wear your letter sweater
Her old man, too. He's got the poetry tic—
So praise his work and you could get in thick.

DORANTE
He hates my Dad! Their libel suit's at bar!

LISETTE
You simpleton. Don't tell him who you *are*.
Suck up to him, make him a happy host.
But find some poem for her, or you are *toast*.
(LISETTE EXITS.)

DORANTE
Oh, sure. Just find a poem. Should be simple...

(DAMIS ENTERS.)

DAMIS
"Descend, O Muse! Unbind thy winding wimple!
Show us thy face in rosy beauty cupp't...!"

DORANTE
Damis! It's me!

DAMIS
No, no. Don't interrupt.
Never before have I been so afire!
I am a rhyming, chiming, sliming (well, not sliming) choir! [*Writes.*]

DORANTE
I'll tell you this: you're not a clairvoyant.

DAMIS
Monsieur, will you please cease your...Christ! *Dorante?!*
(They embrace.)
It's been ten years! How are you? Where've you been?

DORANTE
I thought you went to law school! Didn't get in?

DAMIS
Oh, I got in, then fled those dusty hallways.
How's your old man?

DORANTE
Still blustering, like always.

DAMIS
Your father treated me like your lost brother.

DORANTE
I think he loves you more than my own mother.

DAMIS
But why're you here? Don't tell me! Some romance.

DORANTE
Damis, this one's The One. Don't look askance.
A girl *celestial*, not some dumb coquette.

DAMIS
Her name?

DORANTE
I'd rather not divulge that yet.
Not till I've won my father to my side.
He's got a legal gripe against my bride.

DAMIS
That's all that stands between you? Strife back home?

DORANTE
There's worse. My future wife's a metronome.
Maniac, I mean. About which I know nada.

And now I need a poem as my armada.

DAMIS
Here's luck then, poetry's my new métier!
What would you like? A sonnet? Rondelay?
Haiku? Too arty. Limerick? Too cheap.

DORANTE
I'll tell you what I need. Something with sheep.

DAMIS
Friend, I'm so intimate with sheep it's astral!
I ought to *bleat* my ballads, I'm so pastoral.
(Opens his NOTEBOOK.)
A georgic or an eclogue?

DORANTE
Take your pick.

DAMIS
Here's one half-written that might do the trick.
"Dithyramb To A Lamb."

DORANTE
Great!

DAMIS
Sweet but weighty.
I only need to plug in your fair lady.
So who's this maid? Enumerate her charms,
I'll hang a twangling lyre inside her arms.

DORANTE
You know I've never been too cool with words.

DAMIS
My friend, she's waiting for her wooly herds!
Just free-associate. Pour out some stuff.

DORANTE
She's beautiful...

DAMIS
Stop there! I have enough!
(Scribbles in NOTEBOOK.)
Yes...! Good...! Fantastic...!
(Rips out the POEM and holds it out.)
It's a little rough.

DORANTE
Thank you! Gosh. Sorry to deplete your stock.

The Metromaniacs

DAMIS
(taps his NOTEBOOK)
This quiver's full of arrows. Chock-a-block!
And may I say, continuing the argot,
That my own shafts have found a worthy target...?

DORANTE
You're hinting something.

DAMIS
Am I? Take a whirl.

DORANTE
Don't tell me...!

DAMIS
Yes, I've also found a girl.
"*Celestial*," too, if we're being adjectival.

DORANTE
Wow, that's terrific! (Wait! Have I a rival?)
Who is she?

DAMIS
You won't name your lover true,
So why should I? Oh, all right, here's a clue:
She's here right now beneath this very roof.

DORANTE
Yeah? What's she like?

DAMIS
You might call her...aloof.
Her distance, though, is part of her appeal.

DORANTE
(Damnation! His girl's got to be Lucille!)
Does she like poems?

DAMIS
She writes them night and day.
She has the time, up there, all locked away.
I picture her right now beside her cow...

DORANTE
Her *cow?*

DAMIS
She loves me.

DORANTE
And you know this how?

DAMIS
The site where we two meet: *Parnassus*. [*Shows MAGAZINE.*]

DORANTE
Damn!

DAMIS
I'm sorry...?

DORANTE
Boy, you are a lucky man!
You know, our host here has a well-read child.

DAMIS
Does he?

DORANTE
(He's toying, now, to get me riled.)

DAMIS
If you want more, I'm Cupid at your service.

DORANTE
(Let's see if budding rivals make him nervous.
Yes...! Now I think of it, she said "Damis"!)

DAMIS
What is all this? "To be or not to be"?

DORANTE
Sorry. So tell me, do you know our host?

DAMIS
He shadows me like some adoring ghost.

DORANTE
Why don't you introduce me, just for kicks?

DAMIS
What, Francalou and you? You'd never mix!
The man's a dilettante! A would-be poet!
A dimestore-rhymester "artist," quote unquo-et.
Oh, he's a lovely man, don't get me wrong.
Generous and open, sunshine all day long.
But then in middle age he gets this itch
And now he writes the world's most hopeless kitsch!

Oh, sure, he'll say he wrote it "for a laugh"—
Then make you sit through every lumbering gaffe.
Tonight we're putting on his so-called "play"...?
But wait. I see him coming. Run away!

(FRANCALOU ENTERS with LISETTE.)

FRANCALOU
You turn your back and everything goes bust!
My play, my whole production—in the dust!

DAMIS
Oh no.

FRANCALOU
    Without the kindness to alert me
Three actors pick this moment to desert me!
He playing the servant fell and cut his head;
Our lover caught the pox; our uncle's dead.

DAMIS
The nerve.

FRANCALOU
    Just kicks the bucket, matter-of-factly!

DAMIS
He couldn't wait?

FRANCALOU
    My sentiments exactly.
Have you a grumpy uncle I could use?

DAMIS
I have a grumpy uncle in Toulouse...

FRANCALOU
I bring together family, friends and beaus,
I write a play for Lucy—and we close!
Of course I only wrote it for a laugh.
Still, there are passages of golden chaff.
Like this, for instance...[*Prepares to recite.*]

DAMIS
NO!

FRANCALOU
    The first act climax.

DORANTE
I'd love to hear.

DAMIS
I'll wait for it in iMax.

FRANCALOU
The show is off, why shouldn't I recite?

DAMIS
Because I've solved your nasty casting plight!
A servant you can pluck from those who hover.
Any old grouch could be the uncle's cover.

FRANCALOU
You're playing the nephew. *You* can't play Dorante.

DORANTE
"*Dorante*"?

FRANCALOU
The missing character I want.
The role calls for a handsome, sporty sort.
A hunk in love. Your classic swain, in short.

DAMIS
Then, sir, you have right here the swain you want.
Please meet my dear old friend—

DORANTE
Eraste.

DAMIS
"*Eraste*"?

DORANTE
I'm yours, sir, if you think I've got the stuff.

FRANCALOU
If you're a friend of Cosmo's, that's enough.

DORANTE
Who's Cosmo?

FRANCALOU
Who is Cosmo, says your buddy.

DAMIS
He's acting! See? How's that for a quick study?

FRANCALOU
(arm around Damis's shoulder)
I'd marry this man, sir—were he a girl.

The Metromaniacs   29

When he starts rhapsodizing? Mother-of-pearl!

DORANTE
But what of *your* work, sir? Oh, geez! Oh, *man*!

FRANCALOU
You like my work?

DORANTE
I'm just your biggest fan.
Why else would I be here if not for you?
Your, your, your…adverbs, and your…commas …? *Whoo!*

FRANCALOU
It just so happens I've a brand-*new* play…
[*Produces MANUSCRIPT.*]

DORANTE
Oh, may we hear it?

DAMIS
Maybe Saturday?

FRANCALOU
I only wrote it for a laugh, of course.
It's on the death of Alexander's horse.
"*Bucephalus: A Dirge In Seven Acts.*"

DORANTE
Genius!

FRANCALOU
Some of the rhymes are not un-lax.

DORANTE
The rhymes? I thought you said it was a play.

FRANCALOU
Well, aren't all plays composed in verse today?

DORANTE
Just kidding! Now, about this open part…?

FRANCALOU
Can you portray a swain who's lost his heart?
Was your soul ever slain by love's disdain?
One must first live to feel, and feel to feign!

DORANTE
I'm sorry, what was that again? More slowly?

FRANCALOU
You have to've lived a part to act it wholly.

DORANTE
Then search no further, sir. I *am* this role!
For she who is my life, my love, my soul
(Into Damis's face:)
LOVES SOMEONE ELSE! I swear, disdain's my curse!
My girl, who *is* a poem, is averse!

FRANCALOU
I like you.

DORANTE
Thank you.

FRANCALOU
And you've won the part!
(To LISETTE:)
One costume, madam! Something trim and smart
For—sorry, you're...?

DORANTE
Eraste.

LISETTE
Sir, how d'you do.

DORANTE
(slipping her the POEM Damis wrote)
(And if you'd slip this poem to You-Know-Who...)

(MONDOR ENTERS.)

MONDOR
Another inch, sir, and I'll cut your gullet!
You'll never win my lady-love, you mullet!

FRANCALOU
Now this is drama of the brightest pan!
But wait! Could you impersonate a man?

MONDOR
A man?

FRANCALOU
A servant, in a modest part?

MONDOR
Depends what kind of servant.

FRANCALOU
Honest. Smart.

MONDOR
Monsieur, you have described my inner twin!
But *act*...?

FRANCALOU
I'd pay you half a crown.

MONDOR
I'm in!

FRANCALOU
A servant's rig for this enthusiast.
Locate our uncle and our show is cast!

LISETTE
One lackey outfit and one love-sick pup.
(Quietly, to DORANTE:)
(You soften Francalou, I'll follow up.)
(LISETTE EXITS.)

DORANTE
But, sir, you've some new masterwork to share?

FRANCALOU
You really want to hear it?

DAMIS
No.

DORANTE
Yes. Where?
Where should we go to bask in your, um...

FRANCALOU
Strophes?

DORANTE
Exactly.

FRANCALOU
Cosmo?

DAMIS
Sir, poetic trophies
Like yours deserve a really small recital.
Let me be satisfied with that bold title,
"*Bucephalus*"! Which none dare call cliché.

FRANCALOU
(to DORANTE)
It seems it's you and me, then.

DORANTE
Lead the way!

(FRANCALOU EXITS WITH DORANTE.)

MONDOR
I said there's more bad news? It's Judgment Day.
(FRANCALOU RE-ENTERS.)

FRANCALOU
You're absolutely sure…?

DAMIS
I wish I could!
Your new work no doubt redefines what's "good,"
But, umm, some friends have sought my legal wisdom
Since I've connections in our legal system.

FRANCALOU
I only thought…it's new…you'd want to hear…

DAMIS
But is it true, sir? Meriadec is here?

FRANCALOU
Where did you hear that?

MONDOR
Oh, that's just a rumor.

FRANCALOU
(confidentially)
In fact—it's fact!

DAMIS & MONDOR
She's here?

FRANCALOU
Though, given her humor,
And out of tact, of course she's *incognito*—
Lest someone recognize our famed mosquito.

DAMIS
Mosquito? She's a giant, by your leave!
You know her? Oh, sir, may I touch your sleeve?

The Metromaniacs 33

FRANCALOU
You mean you *like* the work of Meriadec...?
Don't find it muddled, self-indulgent dreck?

DAMIS
Muddled? Of course it's muddled! But *refulgent!*
Oh, God, would I were half as self-indulgent!
The way she'll chronicle her every pimple?
That's poetry's future! Spewing, pure and simple!

FRANCALOU
You sound like this Damis, priest of her credo.

DAMIS
He is nearby.

FRANCALOU
Damis's here?

DAMIS & MONDOR
Incognito.

FRANCALOU
Monsieur de Cosmos, I go pink with shame,
That he, a poet so dim, so dull, so lame,
Would share my house with you, who glow so brightly.

DAMIS
To tell the truth, I know him more than slightly.
We two have been inseparable since birth.

FRANCALOU
Damis? That scribbling dribbler? Of no worth
Except perhaps to lick your wingèd shoe?
If anyone's refulgent, sir, it's *you*.
He's second drawer! No, third! A whining jerk!

DAMIS
I find a few good lines amongst his work.

FRANCALOU
And you think Meriadec's has got a kernel?

DAMIS
It's fertile as the spring, and as eternal!
Beside her, Sappho and Propertius cloy!

FRANCALOU
Watch out, or you might turn her head. *Dear boy!*
[*Embraces DAMIS.*]

DAMIS
Please, may I meet her, sir? I thrill! I thrum!

FRANCALOU
I'll think on it. But listen—keep this mum.

(FRANCALOU EXITS.)

DAMIS
She's here...! She's actually in this house! I'm numb!

MONDOR
Well, now hear this and you'll be numb-er, chum.

DAMIS
First, though, I need to step in for Dorante.
I'll write his father, old Monsieur Geronte! [*Starts writing.*]

MONDOR
Monsieur Damis—DISASTER FROM AFAR!

DAMIS
(writing)
"*Your son's in love but there's some legal bar...*"

MONDOR
You're listening?

DAMIS
No.

MONDOR
Hang up your wingèd shoes.
Judge *Baliveau*'s arrived here from Toulouse.
Your grumpy Uncle Baliveau?

DAMIS
Your point?

MONDOR
He's come to Paris, pal! He cased your joint!
The guy who these ten years paid your tuition?
(My God, this is a lot of exposition!)
You think he found those law books he endowed?
A law degree or *license*, Mister Cloud?
The only license you got is poetic
And Baliveau hates anything ass-thetic.

DAMIS
(rips LETTER out of NOTEBOOK)
Mondor, this letter goes with all due grease

The Metromaniacs 35

To one Monsieur Geronte, rue St. Sulpice.
A missive that will fix Dorante for good.

MONDOR
"Fix him"?

DAMIS
For good.

MONDOR
Well, primo. Understood.
But what about rich uncle? Your response?
Besides this empty show of nonchalance?

DAMIS
Have you forgotten? Where've you been? *Beirut*?

MONDOR
Forgotten what?

DAMIS
My play! *The Talking Flute!*
You think when uncle sees I've got a hit
He'll mind his loot, or what I've done with it?
He'll only heap my head, and yours, with more!
Tonight our fate will change at eight, Mondor!
Just take that letter for me, off you go,
And have no fear of Justice Baliveau.
He'll never find me anyway! We're safe!

(DAMIS EXITS one way with MONDOR as FRANCALOU ENTERS the other way with BALIVEAU.)

FRANCALOU
Baliveau, you arrive here like some waif.

BALIVEAU
I'm on a mission, you might say. I chafe,
While you're the same old temper: *tally-ho*!

FRANCALOU
It comes of seeing you here, Baliveau.
Give us a hug and *then* you can be vexed.

BALIVEAU
Is that a *forest* there? Good Lord, what next?

FRANCALOU
It's for my play tonight—a one-night run.
You're going to come, and love it, and have *fun*!

BALIVEAU
I wish I could work up the proper glee.
My mission here 's my nephew, one Damis.

FRANCALOU
The poet?

BALIVEAU
Don't tell me you know the knave.

FRANCALOU
Not face to face.

BALIVEAU
He'll put me in my grave.
Ten years he's been here—studying Law, I thought—
I come and learn he's *in* debt *and* untaught,
A vagabond to whom a home's abhorrent.
That's why I'm here! I want to get a warrant,
I want him locked up as an arrant thief.
You're well connected. Will you aid my brief?

FRANCALOU
A warrant for a poet? I'd find that hard.
Even Damis, who's not my favorite bard...
But you're my friend, so—yes! He'll be bastille'd!

BALIVEAU
We'll have to find him first. He's gone afield.
For all I know he's clubbing on the Lido.

FRANCALOU
But he's right *here*!

BALIVEAU
My nephew?

FRANCALOU
Incognito.
By great good luck we've one de Cosmos here.
He knows your nephew, *and* (be of good cheer)
Has legal friends who'll sign the proper paper!
It's fixed! I'll put de Cosmos on this caper—
Though I've a tit-for-tat.

BALIVEAU
It's done. Just say.

FRANCALOU
Take on the grumpy uncle in my play.

The Metromaniacs

BALIVEAU
You're joking.

FRANCALOU
Not at all!

BALIVEAU
I, act onstage?

FRANCALOU
A justice from Toulouse who's just your age?
You only have to stand there to be he!
And howl a bit. [*HE HOWLS, demonstrating.*]

BALIVEAU
I have my dignity.

FRANCALOU
Who knows you here? Besides, you *are* this fellow!
For shield, we'll call you *Signor Pirandello*.

BALIVEAU
I'd be ungrateful not to play along.
But in return you'll help me right my wrong?

FRANCALOU
Damis is toast!

(*LISETTE ENTERS.*)

LISETTE
Monsieur...Sorry, you're busy.

FRANCALOU
Lisette, no, here's our howling uncle!
(*BALIVEAU tries to HOWL.*)

LISETTE
Is he?

(*BALIVEAU howls.*)

FRANCALOU
(*gives BALIVEAU a SCRIPT*)
Just learn your lines by eight. No rush, no pressure!

BALIVEAU
I'll try. Your elfin wood should give me leisure
To practice howling to my heart's content.

FRANCALOU
Yes, good! Let fly! I want to hear you vent!

(BALIVEAU EXITS into "the wood.")

LISETTE
They're costumed, sir, the lackey and the gent.

BALIVEAU
(in "the wood")
Aaaaaaaaaahhhhhh!

LISETTE
A tart addition to our juicy gig.
Now I should get into my Lucy rig
To play your daughter.

FRANCALOU
                    Things are coalescing.
Now gods of drama, give us all your blessing!

(DORANTE ENTERS unnoticed, and slips behind a "tree." He is now dressed in a "lover" costume.)

DORANTE
(I'll listen in, see how my suit's progressing.)

BALIVEAU
Ahhhhhhh!

(BALIVEAU howls, startling DORANTE.)

FRANCALOU
Oh, God, I love my daughter so, Lisette.
If she could find a mate I'd pirouette.
You're not acquainted with some handy beau?

LISETTE
Why not de Cosmos?

DORANTE
(*WHAT?!*)

LISETTE
(explaining, as FRANCALOU hears that)
                    Your madman.

FRANCALOU
                                      Oh.

(During the following, we're aware of DORANTE in silent, writhing agony, listening in from the "wood.")

LISETTE
You like de Cosmos and his buoyant style.

FRANCALOU
I would joy to march that couple up the aisle.
I can't imagine any better match!

LISETTE
He's isn't rich...

FRANCALOU
    Who cares? I've got the scratch!
I'll be his in-law patron, make him natty.
What sweeter pastime than play sugar daddy?
I'll buy him robes to put a pocket in!

LISETTE
Sir, if you like this plan then lock it in—
Before Miss Lucy falls for some fine churl
Who as too often happens *has* a girl.
This what's-his-name you just put in your cast...?

FRANCALOU
Dorante?

LISETTE
    You *know* that he's Dorante...?

FRANCALOU
    Eraste?

LISETTE
Eraste! A wealthy guy, attractive, steady.
But I have heard that he's in love already.

FRANCALOU
He mentioned some young miss, and how he feels.

LISETTE
Should Lucy fall for *him*, head over heels...

FRANCALOU
She'd find his heart was pledged—

LISETTE
    —and hers would break.

FRANCALOU
I must prevent that, for my Lucy's sake.

LISETTE
I urge you, disallow him. I *insist*.

FRANCALOU
Well thought, Lisette. It's done. His name's dismissed.
I'll go tell her right now he's off the list!

(FRANCALOU EXITS. DORANTE steps forward.)

LISETTE
Speak of the devil.

DORANTE
Devil, dear, yourself.
What are you *thinking*, evil demon *ELF*?
Who *are* you? Lobbyist for my competition,
Monsieur de Cosmos? Aiding his position
While flushing me straight down the lover's loo?

LISETTE
What are you, nuts? I did all that for *you*!

DORANTE
Who, me? Who you just helped disqualify?
And you stand there and look me in the eye?

LISETTE
If you want Lucy, sir, you have to trust me.

DORANTE
Oh, sure! When I just overheard you bust me?

LISETTE
My masterstroke.

DORANTE
To diss me? It's absurd!

LISETTE
I've culled you from this hundred-headed herd!
She'll *race* for you once you're out of the running—
And *shun her Daddy's choice!* Is that not cunning?

DORANTE
Just tell Lucille I love her. Bang, I'm made!

LISETTE
I don't know why I bother lending aid

To men so stupid they need help to fart.
Monsieur, this isn't craft I'm doing, it's *ART*.

DORANTE
Yes, where's that poem gone since I wangled it?

LISETTE
The thing worked like a charm. I dangled it—
And Lucy grabbed it from my hand by force.
Needless to say, I didn't reveal the source.

DORANTE
She doesn't know the poem's from *me*? Why not?!

LISETTE
Suspense, monsieur! The heart and soul of plot!
She's coming.

DORANTE
What'll I say?

LISETTE
Say nothing. *Stumm*.
You bow, then go away and leave me room.

(LUCILLE ENTERS with the poem DORANTE gave LISETTE.)

LUCILLE
Lizzie, this poem's, like, exquisite. Sublime...!

(DORANTE bows to LUCILLE, moves to exit, comes back, gestures, about to speak, then EXITS as LISETTE motions him off.)

LISETTE
Now *there's* a cavalier who's in his prime.

LUCILLE
Not very verbal. What is he, a mime?

LISETTE
My amorous pick, if *I* were forced to vote.

LUCILLE
He seemed okay, as far as I could note...
And anyway my amorous ballot's cast.
Daddy forbade me someone named Eraste.

LISETTE
No!

LUCILLE
Yeah.

LISETTE
The handsome swain who's in his play?

LUCILLE
I've never seen the guy, I couldn't say.
Anyway, Daddy made him sound so bad
I'm half-inclined to wed the lethal cad.

LISETTE
("bursts into tears")
Forgive me, Miss! I didn't mean it! Honest!

LUCILLE
Forgive you, why?

LISETTE
For praising that Adonis! [i.e., DORANTE.]
I thought he had the right ingredients!
I never meant to foster disobedience.
Forget you ever saw him. Subject closed.

LUCILLE
That was Eraste?

LISETTE
The dude your Dad deposed.

LUCILLE
As I remember now, he's kinda cute...

LISETTE
You guessed he wrote that poem. You're so *astute*.

LUCILLE
That guy composed my dazzling dithyramb?
Be still my heart and fluttering diaphragm!
What's weird is that he writes just like Damis.

LISETTE
All right, Miss. I can tell you now. He's *he*.

LUCILLE
Who he?

LISETTE
The fellow in the cast, who passed?

The Metromaniacs 43

LUCILLE
That's guy's Damis?! You mean…?

LISETTE
Damis's *Eraste*.

LUCILLE
He penned these tropes, these metaphors, these puns?
And then he has those legs, those thighs, those buns?
O fallen star from constellation Ursa!
They're one and the same?

LISETTE
And vice-a-versa.

LUCILLE
I'm dizzy, Liz. And Daddy, please stand clear!

LISETTE
(I think Dorante can pick things up from here.)
But listen, he might stroll by any sec,
So show some girlitude. All tits on deck!

LUCILLE
I look a mess…!

LISETTE
Calm down. This won't go south.
You've got a weapon handy. Do *The Mouth*.

LUCILLE
The Mouth?

LISETTE
(puffs her lips as models do)
The Mouth. It shows you're really lusting.
Lean in and pucker up.

LUCILLE
Liz, that's disgusting.

LISETTE
Miss Lucy, he's a man! Forget the term!
It's stupid stuff like that that makes 'em squirm.
Try it.
(LUCILLE does THE MOUTH.)
That's great. Don't worry, I can kibbitz.
He's coming! Better plump all your exhibits.

(LUCILLE EXITS, MONDOR ENTERS from another way.)

MONDOR
All right, where is he? Lead me to the swine!

LISETTE
You have to leave.

MONDOR
You're not Dorante's! You're mine!

LISETTE
You have to leave!

MONDOR
(produces PISTOLS)
You see these guns?

LISETTE
They're fake.

MONDOR
Well, I'll still wave 'em!

LISETTE
Go, for heaven's sake!

MONDOR
Who needs them anyhow? We're stuck like glue!
My boss gets Lucy—I inherit you!

LISETTE
Your master isn't in the running.

MONDOR
No?
Your boss has not decided he's her beau?
The future pusher of her baby's pram?

LISETTE
I thought your master's named...

MONDOR
Damis.

LISETTE
Oh, *damn!*
So he's de Cosmos?

MONDOR
They're one and the same.

The Metromaniacs   45

LISETTE
Well, thanks for really screwing up my game!

MONDOR
You want to slip your man in, please don't bother.
See, my boss wrote Geronte, Dorante's old father.
To step on him, he said. Dorante gets nixed,
My master wins, your boy gets 86'd,
You and I are one. How does that re-tune you?

LISETTE
If I had time I'd bare my butt and moon you.
Now go!

(MONDOR EXITS. LISETTE puts the PISTOLS aside. DORANTE ENTERS and goes to LUCILLE.)

DORANTE
(bows)
   I am Dorante.

LUCILLE
   You mean Eraste?
[*She does The Mouth.*]

DORANTE
I...What? Oh, yes, "Eraste"! You see, I'm cast
As one "Dorante" and had forgot myself.

LUCILLE
Oh, sir, you can put pretence on the shelf. [*Does The Mouth.*]
I know your true identity. [*Mouth.*] I'm wise. [*Mouth.*]

DORANTE
I'm sorry...?

LUCILLE
   Who you are? [*Mouth.*] Minus disguise? [*Mouth.*]

DORANTE
I'm still at sea.

LUCILLE
   So fine. We'll leave it moot. [*Mouth.*]
Your need for anonymity's acute.

DORANTE
Because of that old pending libel suit?

LUCILLE
Monsieur, we seem to be two passing ships.
(Does The Mouth more aggressively.)

DORANTE
Do you have some affliction of the lips?

LUCILLE
I'm *lusting*.

DORANTE
For?

LUCILLE
A certain poet!

DORANTE
Oh?

LUCILLE
You do know who composed this bright morceau.
[*Shows POEM.*]

DORANTE
I'll kill him!

LUCILLE
Who?

DORANTE
The source of that debris.

LUCILLE
Monsieur, I mean the man I love. *Damis...?*

DORANTE
I'll massacre the dog!

LUCILLE
The what?

DORANTE
Him!

LUCILLE
Who?
Monsieur, my pointed reference was to *you*!
The author of my dithyrambic lamb?

DORANTE
I will not lie to you, nor fiddle, nor sham.
I did not write that poem.

LUCILLE
Oh, don't be coy.

DORANTE
I read the sports page!

LUCILLE
Don't be such a boy.

And Meriadec?

DORANTE
What's that?

LUCILLE
Your love's bestower?

Will you just throw her over?

DORANTE
I don't know her!

LUCILLE
Nobody does.

DORANTE
They say that love's insane.
This conversation's knotting up my brain!
I don't write poems, I flunked French twice, I'm stupid!
But I've been visited by Mr. Cupid
And thanks to naked baby this is true:
I *love* you. *I* love *you*. You. Me. I. You.
That's it! That's all I got! I'm done, I'm mute!

LUCILLE
I hate to say this but you're very cute.
So if you want me I'll be by some tree...

(LUCILLE does The Mouth over her shoulder and goes off into "the wood." LISETTE comes forward and accosts DORANTE.)

LISETTE
So who's unhappy now?

DORANTE
I'll tell you: *me*.
She loves that poem's author!

LISETTE
Yes! You're he!

DORANTE
Except I'm not!

LISETTE
She's got the fatal yen!
You should be blissful!

DORANTE
But how can I when
She'll find out I'm a fiction, I'm a fake?

LISETTE
When *isn't* love, thank God, one big mistake?

DORANTE
I did, right in the middle, get the yips.
You know she does this weird thing with her lips?

LISETTE
Desire.

DORANTE
Thanks to a gift I don't possess.
So now I'm rival to...myself, I guess!
Plus Cosmo/slash/Damis, lord of misrule—
Who I'm convinced is playing me for a fool.
Maybe you're playing me, too, to make me writhe.

LISETTE
Monsieur Dorante, you're lucky I'm so blithe.
I have been slaving as *your confidante*,
Not as a spy for some an*ti*-Dorante,
And, you may notice, doing all this for *free!*

LUCILLE
(in "the wood")
Eraste...?

DORANTE
She's calling someone. Oh, it's me.
I'm going to have my eye on you, so watch it.

LISETTE
I help devise this plan and then you'd botch it?

DORANTE
Maybe you date him, work in symphony.

The Metromaniacs 49

LISETTE
This date, monsieur, will live in infamy!
And so of course you realize: this means *war*!

DORANTE
We'll see which suitor's side you're working for.
All right, it's war! To death! At any cost!

(DORANTE joins LUCILLE in "the wood.")

LISETTE
I have to change...

(MONDOR ENTERS, now in a flashy servant's livery.)

MONDOR
How's this?

LISETTE
(from twenty feet away)
                    Slap!

MONDOR
                              OW!

LISETTE
                              Get lost!

(LISETTE EXITS one way.)

MONDOR
I know you're only putting on this frost!

(DAMIS ENTERS another way.)

DAMIS
So did you take my note to St. Sulpice?

MONDOR
I might have. Or might not.

DAMIS
               What's this? Caprice?
Since when does "servant" mean the disobeying one?

MONDOR
In this [*i.e., his costume*] I'm not a servant, I'm just playing one.
I'm not even here! I only *seem* to be.

DAMIS
Would I could only *seem* to be Damis

Since being him only brings me indigestion.
Damis or not Damis.

DAMIS & MONDOR
That is the question.

DAMIS
(sits on a "rock." It's foam, and deflates beneath him.)
I searched for Meriadec. Does she exist?

MONDOR
Maybe this broad's like you: a kind of *mist*.

DAMIS
Would we two even be simpatico?
Were she like Francalou...upbeat, aglow...
If she had his élan, his verve, his vim.

MONDOR
Forget this Meriadec. Just marry *him!*

DAMIS
Mondor, I'll do it?

MONDOR
Marry him?

DAMIS
Forget her.
I'm sorry I ever met, well, never met her.
My Shepherdess, 'twas lovely but farewell!

MONDOR
Too bad, just when you two were doing so swell.
Hey, why not find a person of her sex
And substitute her face for Meriadec's?

DAMIS
Yes...! Find some random proxy to adore...!
I sometimes marvel at your sense, Mondor.
Just pick a stand-in! Excellent! But who?

MONDOR
Have you checked out Miss Lucy Francalou?
Pink dress, gold hair?

DAMIS
Exploit my host? No thanks.

The Metromaniacs

MONDOR
She is his heir, sir, and you got no francs.
Plus did you know she's nutso for fine verse?
She reads it, writes it—*and* comes with a purse.
Plus *plus*: her father, on crusade for her,
Is telling everyone you're made for her!

DAMIS
All right, where is she?

MONDOR
        You wait here, I'll check.
(MONDOR EXITS one way. FRANCALOU ENTERS another.)

FRANCALOU
My friend, I've just communed with Meriadec.

DAMIS
Where is she?!

FRANCALOU
       She's so close you two could peck.
But by the by, have you yet met my child?

DAMIS
I haven't had the pleasure...(Wait. That's wild.
Lucille writes poetry. Meriadec as well...)
You're close to Meriadec?

FRANCALOU
        As nut to shell.

DAMIS
(I think he's throwing out a tentacle.)

FRANCALOU
So close we're practically identical.

DAMIS
(That's it! Lucille is Meriadec for sure!)

FRANCALOU
I'll try to find her, and...[*Shakes hands.*] Good luck, monsieur!

(FRANCALOU EXITS.)

DAMIS
That's why Mondor was pushing me. He *knew!*
But hid it from me, as did Francalou.
Meriadec's Lucy, not off in some hut!

(LISETTE ENTERS, dressed as Lucille for the play.)

LISETTE/LUCILLE
(I ought to pass in this...)

DAMIS
Stay, goddess!

LISETTE/LUCILLE
What?

DAMIS
Mad Shepherdess!

LISETTE/LUCILLE
I'm sorry...?

DAMIS
Is it you?
O, bliss! It's you, who like celestial dew
Silver each daisy through your argent art!
As it is you who own my ardent heart!

LISETTE/LUCILLE
Well, 'bye...

DAMIS
Ye GODS, must we two live in twain?
Who are one heart, one soul, a single bwain?

LISETTE/LUCILLE
Brain?

DAMIS
Brain.
To think I thought I loved you up to now!
To think I thought you owned a cow!

LISETTE/LUCILLE
A cow?
Yeah, look, I gotta sprint...

DAMIS
Oh, drop this role.
I know who you are in your deepest soul.
Your secret's out, thanks to your father's spiel.

LISETTE/LUCILLE
My father...?

DAMIS
Yes.

LISETTE/LUCILLE
(He thinks that I'm Lucille!)

DAMIS
Another hint. Does "Peauduncqville" ring bells?
Those rabid rhymes, those violent villanelles?
Since I first read your work I've been a wreck.

LISETTE
I see...(He also thinks I'm *Meriadec!*)

DAMIS
May Pegasus the Wingèd never fly,
May all the streams of Hippocrene run dry,
If I don't pledge my soul to you—forever.

LISETTE/LUCILLE
(aping Lucille)
Yeah, well...That's cool...Why not, I mean...Whatever.
(FRANCALOU ENTERS.)

FRANCALOU
Lucille...

LISETTE/LUCILLE
(turns away)
Yeah, Dad?

FRANCALOU
You two have met, then. Good.

DAMIS
I love your Lucy, sir!

FRANCALOU
And so you should!

DAMIS
You didn't tell me of her secret, though.

FRANCALOU
The real Lucille beneath the surface? No.
And may you two find bliss unto the last!
Now, I've just penned a poem that has surpassed...

LISETTE/LUCILLE
You know who'd like to hear that, Dad? Eraste.

FRANCALOU
You're absolutely right. He'll go berserk.

(FRANCALOU EXITS.)

LISETTE
(That'll pay back Dorante for being a jerk.)

DAMIS
Lucy, we are a knot no blade can sever.

LISETTE/LUCILLE
Yeah, hey...Why not, I mean...That's cool...Whatever...

(THEY EXIT. As they do, DAMIS drops his NOTEBOOK. MONDOR ENTERS.)

MONDOR
You dropped your notebook, sir! [*To US:*] Boy, am I clever?
Look at him! Tight already with our heiress,
Like he's the greatest gigolo in Paris!
Maybe this poetry really works on chicks.
Let's see here, maybe I'll pick up some tricks...

(He studies the NOTEBOOK as DORANTE and LUCILLE ENTER from "the wood.")

LUCILLE
O, sweet Damis! I can't believe it's true!

MONDOR
(reads from NOTEBOOK)
Mad Shepherdess!

LUCILLE
I'm sorry...?

MONDOR
Is it you?
O, bliss! It's you, who like celestial dew
Silver each daisy through your argent art!
As it is you who own my ardent heart!

LUCILLE
Sir, you're a poet?

MONDOR
Not yet a paying one.

LUCILLE
You're not a servant?

MONDOR
No, just playing one.

DORANTE
Lucille...

MONDOR
Ye GODS, must we two live in twain?
Who are one heart, one soul, a single bwain?

LUCILLE
Brain?
What glorious words! Like sun from warming south!

MONDOR
(I think she likes me.)
(Yeah, she's doing *The Mouth!*)
But wait a sec, now wait a sec. Who's he?
Didn't I just see you float off with Damis?

LUCILLE
He *is* Damis.

MONDOR
Who, *he*?

LUCILLE
(to DORANTE)
Aren't you?

DORANTE
Who, me?

MONDOR
This jock, this creep? Damis? Don't make me laugh.
He wouldn't know a sheep from a giraffe.

LUCILLE
(to DORANTE)
Show him! Well? Rhapsodize! Play your pan-pipes!

MONDOR
I wouldn't use this piker's poems for hand-wipes.

LUCILLE
Go on!

DORANTE
Behold, forsooth! A leaping bock!

MONDOR
Don't strain yourself. No, really. Take a rock—
While I shoot coruscating phrases toward the skies
So luminous, you'll have to shield your eyes!

LUCILLE
Be still, my heart! I know that style and tone!
Such eloquence could be Damis's alone!
(Notices the NOTEBOOK and looks inside.)
Look at these odes! I recognize the script...
And look, here's where my lilting lamb was ripped!

DORANTE
I have an explanation.

LUCILLE
Well, unroll it.

DORANTE
That poem, the one I sent to you...?

MONDOR
He stole it.

DORANTE
Shall I run for a sword? Feed you its blade?

MONDOR
Go run and finish fiddling with her maid.

LUCILLE
My *maid*?!

DORANTE
Lisette?

LUCILLE
Lisette.

MONDOR
(This oughta show her.)

LUCILLE
Next explanation, please.

DORANTE
Okay, I know her.

LUCILLE
(from several feet away)
Slap!

DORANTE
OW!

LUCILLE
(to MONDOR)
So you're Damis.

MONDOR
Here in the flesh.

LUCILLE
I love you!

MONDOR
Well then, hey, what say we mesh?

(LUCILLE kisses him hard.)

DORANTE
I know what's going on here. I'm not blind!

LUCILLE
I thought I loved you. Oh, well. Never mind.
(To MONDOR:)
You want me? I'll be splayed beneath a tree.

(LUCILLE goes off into the "wood," doing The Mouth over her shoulder.)

DORANTE
I know who masterminded this. DAMIS...!?

(DORANTE starts to run off, but FRANCALOU ENTERS.)

FRANCALOU
Ah, there you are!

DORANTE
Who, me?

FRANCALOU
Where've you been hiding?
I hear you want to hear what I've been writing.

DORANTE
Says who?

FRANCALOU
You don't?

DORANTE
You see...I have to go...

FRANCALOU
It isn't long. Three thousand lines or so.
I wrote it for a laugh.

DORANTE
No, please, sir...NO...!

(FRANCALOU leads DORANTE off.)

MONDOR
(to US)
Now here's a comfy place to take a pause...

(DAMIS ENTERS from the "wood.")

DAMIS
Mondor—Mondor, I am in Cupid's jaws.

MONDOR
Well, luckily for you the kid is toothless.

DAMIS
So this is love! Ecstatic! Vatic! Ruthless!
I've never known its like, my stout auxiliar.

BALIVEAU
(from "the wood")
Aaaaaaaah!

MONDOR
Jesus!

DAMIS
Wait. That voice sounded familiar.

MONDOR
Monsieur, I'm holding here for wild applause.

LISETTE
Yoo-hoo!
(DAMIS goes into the wood)

MONDOR
So like I say, we'll take a pause...

DORANTE
(entering)
I'll kill you! Though I can't recall the cause...

MONDOR
What, understand this *plot?* Sir, life's too brief.

DORANTE
So I don't have to think? That's a relief.
Wait—yes, I have to think! And win Lucille!
So bring it on! Whatever the ordeal!

FRANCALOU
(entering, reading)
"*Thus Alexander conquered all Punjabi...*"

(DORANTE runs out, followed by FRANCALOU.)

MONDOR
Now for that pause. Feel free to crowd the lobby
And puzzle out our plot with alcohol.
So who am I again...?

LUCILLE
(cooing, from the "wood")
            Damis...!

MONDOR
            I'm coming, doll!

(MONDOR lifts to his mouth a pair of imaginary pan-pipes and we hear him playing as he EXITS into "the wood," dancing like Pan.)

CURTAIN

END OF ACT ONE

ACT TWO

(The same, a while later. MONDOR ENTERS.)

MONDOR
Welcome back, all, from coffee and the pot!
All gadgets off? Good! Let's review our plot.
This guy looks worried. No, there'll be no quiz.
Let's just tote up where everybody is.
First, splayed upon our forest's bosky floor,
Lucille is picnicking with me, Mondor—
Though she thinks I'm Damis, her rhyming hero.
The odds I'm gonna clear that up? Um—zero.

LUCILLE
(from the "wood")
More caviar, darling?

MONDOR
Just a pinch, my finch.

LUCILLE
A sip of brandy...?

MONDOR
I could stand an inch.

(They do The Mouth to each other and LUCILLE EXITS into the "wood.")

MONDOR (CONT'D)
Judge Baliveau, a foe with razor tines,
Is in a thicket memorizing lines...

BALIVEAU
"Aaaaaaahhhhhhh!"

MONDOR
...howling from time to time without much talent.
Dorante, our play's exasperated gallant,
Paces the house...
(DORANTE ENTERS, pacing.)
           ...growling...
(DORANTE growls in frustration.)
                    ...then takes a post...
(DORANTE stands still.)
Then sighs a bit...
(DORANTE sighs miserably.)
           Then tries to flee his host.
(FRANCALOU ENTERS, with MANUSCRIPT.)

FRANCALOU
"*And then Bucephalus, like mighty bronze...*"
Where are you going? "*...amazed the Amazons...*"

(DORANTE EXITS, fleeing, with FRANCALOU following.)

MONDOR
Damis, now one of history's great Don Juans,
Basks in possession of his longed-for pet.

(DAMIS STROLLS THROUGH with LISETTE on his arm.)

DAMIS
You're mine, Lucille!

(DAMIS and LISETTE EXIT.)

MONDOR
        Too bad "Lucille's" Lisette.
Nor let's forget, among our many plot points,
The Talking Flute, [*shows FLYER*] one of our coming hot points.
Tonight it lights the Comédie's marquee.
Damis thinks it'll make him rich. We'll see.
But hark! I hear more plot, thanks to this fellow...

BALIVEAU
(entering from the garden)
"*Aaaaaaahhhhhhhh!*"

(FRANCALOU ENTERS as MONDOR EXITS back into the "wood.")

FRANCALOU
Are you word-perfect, Signor Pirandello?

BALIVEAU
If nothing else today, I've learned to bellow.
And though I did resist I have to say
That I've been truly tickled by your play.

FRANCALOU
It's brilliant?

BALIVEAU
        No! But could be, with a nudge.
And I could swear I know this prickly judge! [*I.e., in the script.*]
In him I see my every flaw, my faults—
He had my stomach doing somersaults—
Yet moved me, as did all your panorama.

FRANCALOU
And there you name the heart and soul of drama:

Empathy, simple empathy for all,
Prickly or unprickly, august or small!
These shades are us! They speak, they act, they fade.
But with some added sauce...

FRANCALOU & BALIVEAU
The sexy maid!

BALIVEAU
Your poet-nephew harrowed me with pity.
I saw Damis—adrift in this cruel city...
Alone and starving, coughing in some bed...
And as I read, Well, *damn* the Law, I said!
Jail my own flesh and blood? It's a disgrace!
When next I meet Damis we shall embrace!

FRANCALOU
Good man! And wait till you rehearse with Cosmos!
When he gets here, you and this judge will osmose!

BALIVEAU
Your Cosmo plays my nephew in the scene?

FRANCALOU
With him for target how your edge will keen!
For life has this in common with performance:
A partner shapes our laughs and shares our torments.
(Glancing into the wings.)
But here comes Cosmo now, let's set the stage.
You're pacing at the top. You're in a rage.

BALIVEAU
"*Ahhhh*"

FRANCALOU
Good, ambush him the moment he appears.
You can't be too extreme.

BALIVEAU
I'll singe his ears!

FRANCALOU
Warm up your instrument. BAA BAA, BO BO.

BALIVEAU
BAA BAA, BO BO.

FRANCALOU
He's coming. Places! *Go!*

(FRANCALOU hides behind a "tree" to observe. DAMIS ENTERS, carrying his script.)

BALIVEAU
"*Ahhhhhhh! So it's you, then, is it?*"

(DAMIS, hearing his uncle's voice, turns away so BALIVEAU can't see his face. BALIVEAU keeps his eyes on his script.)

DAMIS
Waaaah! Uncle! You?

BALIVEAU
"*Yes, it is I, you! Scoundrel come to spew!
My poison! Boy! So this is how. You use me?*"
BAA BAA BO BO, BAA BAA BO BO.

(FRANCALOU slips away with a thumbs-up.)

DAMIS
Excuse me?

BALIVEAU
"*I find you here pursuing a poet's fame,
Not even using your own...*" What's it...

DAMIS
Name?

BALIVEAU
"*...own name?*"
So you don't want to face me?

DAMIS
I'm ashamed.

BALIVEAU
Yes, good! Put on a show of being blamed.

DAMIS
Under the circumstances, sir, I'm reeling.

BALIVEAU
You *should* be, given all you must be feeling!
Surprise. Disgrace at having lost my trust.

DAMIS
Yet hope for mercy, knowing that you're just.
Please, Uncle, I...

BALIVEAU
"Enough! Ungrateful cur!
I've no doubt there's some girl?"

DAMIS
I love her, sir.

BALIVEAU
"Silence! You've wooed the wench! Wepent, repent, in woe!"

DAMIS
(That sounds familiar...) [*Checks his script.*]

DAMIS & BALIVEAU
"Heed my charge—or go!"

BALIVEAU
Wait, that was *my* line. Why're you so amused?

DAMIS
At finding life and theatre so confused...
(*HE turns around.*)
Uncle.

BALIVEAU
Damis! Dear boy! [*Embraces him.*] Is this amazing?

DAMIS
"Amazing," uncle, would be paraphrasing.
And an affectionate embrace? What's this?

BALIVEAU
I've had a total metamorphosis!

DAMIS
So I don't irritate, don't rankle you...?

BALIVEAU
No! Thanks to this mad farce of Francalou.
But why are you here, and what's this *nom de guerre*?

DAMIS
I could ask you the same, please be aware.

BALIVEAU
Now listen...

DAMIS
None of that. You've metamorphed.

BALIVEAU

You're right. My former prickliness being dwarfed,
I here abjure all rage, decry all spats!

DAMIS

We're actors, too, who're nature's democrats.

BALIVEAU

Well, now you're overdoing it a fraction...

DAMIS

Theatre is democracy in action!
It's people gathering, just as in our wood,
To put their minds toward making something *good*.
Each person valuable, each adding gifts.
Imagine, uncle, all the wars, the rifts
We'd heal if life were theatre all the time!
We'd be in costume somewhere! Speaking rhyme!

BALIVEAU

A strong defense, my equal under make-up.
You have a sense for law. [*Getting angry:*]
Why not *wake up*...? So you're amused again?

DAMIS

Because it's droll
The way you bleed right back into your role.

BALIVEAU

Oh, do I.

DAMIS

You're transformed...

BALIVEAU

Damn transformation!
And damn your high-hat insubordination!
Will you give up this Poetry? Well, boy, speak!

DAMIS

We're on page 66. "*To quote the Greek...*"

BALIVEAU

To quote the Greek, you're an ungrateful cur!
So run to ruin! The devil be your spur!
Go crawl with poetry to some lightless crypt!

DAMIS

Well, now we've *really* left behind the script...

BALIVEAU
You were the only good my brother left me.
And see the way you've robbed me, have bereft me
Not just of gold but of a would-be son.
For poems?

DAMIS
            For what great poets have always won:
Glory. You think war's harder, swords more real?
To wield a pen each day takes arms of steel!
For poets take the field against the best—
Sophocles, Shakespeare, Plautus, all the rest
Who quoted by us now make us seem sages!
I want to write the thoughts of future ages.
So yes, I'll study law. The laws of art!
And pass the hardest Bar: the human heart!

BALIVEAU
Take half my fortune now. Take all, I plead!

DAMIS
But there's no call, sir! *This* precludes the need! [*Shows FLYER.*]

BALIVEAU
"*The Talking Flute*"?

DAMIS
           "*The Talking Flute.*"

BALIVEAU
                        What's that?

DAMIS
My handiwork. In gold—a million flat!

BALIVEAU
It says one "Bouillabaisse" composed this piece.

DAMIS
Me! Future owner of the Golden Fleece!

BALIVEAU
Well, isn't this wonderful, tip-top, first-rate!
(*Aside to us:*)
(You see how well I've learned to simulate?
In truth, I'll see to it that this play fails—
And see him off to test our Paris jails!)
(*To DAMIS:*)
But if this flops? That happens, don't forget.

DAMIS
I'm so sure, Uncle, that I'll make a bet.
If my play's not an undiluted smash
I'll give up poetry and trade panache
For Law—no, *tax* law, peak of legal boredom.
I'll pledge my days to greed and legal whoredom.

BALIVEAU
You're on! [*They shake on it.*] But where's this girl?

DAMIS
My heart's ideal?
You'd really like to meet her, sir?—*Lucille!*
She's my host's heir, and spun from eiderdown!

(*LISETTE ENTERS, still dressed as Lucille.*)

LISETTE/LUCILLE
Uh-huh?

DAMIS
Lucille, my uncle's come to town.

LISETTE/LUCILLE
Hi.

BALIVEAU
Meeting you, my dear, my prayers are paid!
(Does he suppose I'm blind? This girl's the *maid!*)

DAMIS
Secretly, sir, she's Meriadec!

BALIVEAU
She's who?
I thought she was Lucille!

DAMIS
She's Lucy, too.
She's no mere human, she's a whole new phylum!

BALIVEAU
To house you two, one needs a whole asylum!

(*DORANTE sneaks into the "wood" again to eavesdrop.*)

LISETTE/LUCILLE
I love Damis, sir. He's, like, so unique.
Just rub his head and you can make him speak.

DAMIS
(as LISETTE/LUCILLE rubs his head)
"By the shores of Gitchee Goomee,
By the shining Big Sea Water..." Keep going!

DORANTE
(She never rubbed *my* head and got me flowing!)

(DORANTE EXITS unnoticed.)

DAMIS
Did you see that, sir? She's a poetry *lever*.

LISETTE/LUCILLE
A pleasure meeting you, Monsieur Whatever.

(LISETTE EXITS.)

DAMIS
Doesn't Lucille just *glow?*

BALIVEAU
She's silver-plated.
But let's not tell our host yet we're related.

DAMIS
Gladly—if you won't tell about my show.
I want to bask in secret in the glow
Of sparkling notices and rave reviews!

BALIVEAU
Your future, nephew, is a lighted fuse.

(FRANCALOU ENTERS.)

FRANCALOU
How goes it here?

BALIVEAU
Oh, very well indeed.
(Privately to FRANCALOU, as THEY START OUT:)
I want that warrant, friend—at double speed!
You said you had some guest with legal traction?

[FRANCALOU is about to say "De Cosmos"...]

BALIVEAU
I don't care who it is. I just want *action!*

(FRANCALOU and BALIVEAU EXIT.)

The Metromaniacs

DAMIS
And all these years my uncle seemed so tart.
Turns out the man's a pussycat at heart!
And what a scene, when we two first collided!
The way truth and illusion coincided.
I'll put it in my notebook...Wait. It's gone.
Dorante asked...Well! How's *that* for goings-on?
Who'd ever think my friend was such a louse
He'd steal my poems for his prospective spouse!

(DORANTE ENTERS.)

DORANTE
Monsieur, I must request you leave this house
Or meet me with a weapon in your hand.

DAMIS
It hardly suits a thief to sound so grand.

DORANTE
I'm a thief?

DAMIS
Hand it over.

DORANTE
What?

DAMIS
My book.

DORANTE
I haven't seen it.

DAMIS
Kleptomaniac!

DORANTE
Crook!

DAMIS
Oh, *I'm* a crook?

DORANTE
With more than rhymes to steal—
So hand her over.

DAMIS
Hand her who?

DORANTE
Lucille!

DAMIS
It's true that we're in love. What's that to you?

DORANTE
To me? The man she pledged her future to?

DAMIS
My Meriadec?

DORANTE
What is a MERIADEC?!

DAMIS
So you don't know.

DORANTE
Know what?

DAMIS
You'd better check.

DORANTE
Look, I am sick and tired of being your dupe—
Yours and our host's and all your comic troupe
Who've hatched this plot to make of me your butt.

DAMIS
I didn't know you knew Lucille!

DORANTE
You *what?*
Look. We had a friendship. Now you'd see it bleed?

DAMIS
She loves my poetry. You can hardly *read*.

DORANTE
Oh, really? I?

DAMIS
Name any writer. One.

DORANTE
Well, William Shake...spool, shaft, stein...can be fun.

DAMIS
I think the facts speak for themselves, my friend.

DORANTE
What *are* the facts?

DAMIS
I'm hers, you're not, The End.
And here she comes to clarify who's who.

(*LUCILLE ENTERS with MONDOR, who carries Damis's NOTEBOOK.*)

DAMIS
We've spoken, sweetie. Tell him.

LUCILLE
Who are you?

DAMIS
She's joking.—Don't you want to rub my head?

LUCILLE
Rub this. [*From a distance:*] *Slap!*

DAMIS
OW!

MONDOR
'Scuse me. Rub mine instead.

(*LUCILLE rubs Mondor's head and he pants like a dog.*)

DAMIS
He has my notebook! Give that back, you clown!
[*Takes NOTEBOOK.*]

MONDOR
(*takes NOTEBOOK back*)
This? Where I've copied my sestinas down?

DAMIS
(*takes NOTEBOOK back*)
Since when does "servant" mean "betraying one"?

LUCILLE
(*takes NOTEBOOK*)
He's not a servant! He's just playing one.
You can't judge Bouillabaisse like some low brute.

DAMIS
Bouillabaise?

MONDOR
Author of...[*He shows the FLYER.*]

DAMIS
The Talking Flute?!
You, you, you worm...You are *vermiculate*!

LUCILLE
And you, monsieur, are inarticulate.
He vanquished me as Caesar conquered Gaul!
Now Bouillabaisse, shall have my heart—and *all*.

MONDOR
C'mon, Poopsie. Let's go finish that champagne.

(LUCILLE and MONDOR EXIT.)

DORANTE
You staged all this! It's part of your campaign!

DAMIS
Staged that? For *what*?

DORANTE
For...reasons...clear as crystals.
But what's this here? A pair of dueling pistols?
Pick one and die or else forever rue it!

DAMIS
I've never faced real death before. I'll do it!

DORANTE
And what've we here? A grove designed for duels!

DAMIS
How do we do it? Do you know the rules?

DORANTE
Three steps and fire is how the precept runs.
Is this thing loaded...?

DAMIS
I'm inept with guns.

DORANTE
Never mind! So! Prepare to enter history.

(They stand back-to-back.)

DAMIS
Thus goes Damis to face the final mystery!
To cross the transcendental Hellespont!

DORANTE
Mother, remember me! I was…

DAMIS
    Dorante.

DORANTE
        …Dorante!
One, two, three!
(They march three steps, turn and fire. We hear a pathetic "pop!")
    DAMN it! That's right! Go on, smirk!
We'll try again—this time with guns that work!

(FRANCALOU ENTERS, with MANUSCRIPT.)

FRANCALOU
Ah, there you are!

DORANTE
    Oh, no…

FRANCALOU
    A chilly greeting.

DORANTE
I bet Lisette urged us to have this meeting…?
(To DAMIS:)
You know? *Lisette*? Your second in this game?

DAMIS
Lisette? I know no person by that name.

DORANTE
You fake! You fraud! You ranting, canting liar!

FRANCALOU
Well! Backstage drama? Trouble in the choir?

DAMIS
There's been some inexplicable snafu.

DORANTE
Like this conspiracy—*which you foreknew*?
Is that what you would call some odd, crossed *WIRE*?!?!

FRANCALOU
Give your Dorante a touch of this same fire.

DORANTE
I *AM* Dorante!

FRANCALOU
You're cast, it's understood.

DORANTE
I mean for real!

FRANCALOU
A method actor. Good!
It seems you're everything de Cosmos says.

DORANTE
You know Lucille's in love with Bouillabaisse?

FRANCALOU
The soup?

DORANTE
The nut! Who's probably his shill! [*i.e., Damis's.*]

FRANCALOU
I know no one named Bouillabaisse.

DORANTE
You will!
The fact is, sir, I love your daughter so.

FRANCALOU
Does she love you?

DORANTE
She did an hour ago—
Till Judas here slipped in and took my place.

FRANCALOU
And then...?

DAMIS
She rubbed my head and slapped my face,
At which my servant stole our Aphrodite.

FRANCALOU
I've never known Lucille to be so flighty.
But good! It means she's showing signs of life!

DORANTE
She's rubbing servants who should be my wife!

FRANCALOU
(reads from his ms.)
"*Act Six, Scene Ten. We hear a Persian fife...*"

DORANTE
Monsieur, this is no time for dramaturgy!
What I need is a ring, and her, and clergy!

DAMIS
You really love her, then? Full out, grand slam?

DORANTE
I *told* you when I begged you for a lamb!

DAMIS
I swear I didn't know.

DORANTE
That is so *lame*.

DAMIS
You never said Lucille was your girl's name.

DORANTE
Oh. *Oh*. That's your excuse? Some pale cliché?

DAMIS
We're like some mini-plot from this man's play!

FRANCALOU
Yes Cosmo, how's your "uncle" in that scene?

DAMIS
So real and so convincing I feel green.
I wonder that you managed to engage him.

FRANCALOU
A dilettantish nephew has enraged him—
Your pal Damis.

DORANTE
His "*PAL*" Damis?! That's *HIM*!!!

FRANCALOU
Monsieur, I know that you're upset, you're grim,
But I've got matters of my own to tend.

(To DAMIS:)
He wondered if you had some legal friend...

DAMIS
Who'd get his nephew dangling from a noose?

FRANCALOU
Oh, I think jail-time's quite enough abuse.
We wouldn't want to loose the law's full torrent!

DAMIS
Let me inquire about the proper warrant
(Though a *smash play* may save our dilettante).
Your servant, sir. And your true friend, Dorante.

(DAMIS EXITS.)

FRANCALOU
A spirit adversity could never daunt!
That's odd. He called you...

DORANTE
                Sir, I *am* Dorante.
Not in your play. I mean Dorante in truth.

FRANCALOU
Son of Geronte?!

DORANTE
                Yes. Blame it on my youth
And on my admiration for your daughter...

FRANCALOU
No, I will blame that pettifogging plotter—
Your father, whose black blots will never dry!
Who on his knees could not indemnify
The time I've lost to legal to-and-fro.
I could have been a poet years ago!

DORANTE
So youth must pay for age's sometime folly?

FRANCALOU
That was quite eloquent.

DORANTE
                Not bad, huh? Golly!

FRANCALOU
Well, damn all eloquence. I've no remorse!
Leave my house!—Well, after the show, of course.

DORANTE

I'm sorry, sir, but I am done with posing.
(DORANTE throws off a piece of his lover costume and EXITS as LISETTE ENTERS, still dressed as Lucille.)

FRANCALOU

Another actor lost!

LISETTE/LUCILLE

Who cares? We're closing.

FRANCALOU

Closing? Before we opened? It's absurd!

LISETTE/LUCILLE

Go chase your guests if you won't take my word.
Some play debuts at the Française tonight [*shows FLYER*]
And, getting wind of it, they all took flight.

(DAMIS ENTERS.)

DAMIS

It's true? They've all run off to my, to this, premiere?

LISETTE/LUCILLE

Some kind of masterpiece, from what I hear.

FRANCALOU

Well, then, we'll have to see this thing first-hand—
Since if it's good, no doubt it will get panned.
"*By Bouillabaisse...*" That somehow rings a bell...

DAMIS

He isn't who you think he is.

FRANCALOU

Well, hell,
Who is? Let's catch this while it's still on view.

DAMIS

I'll wait, with better hopes for it than you.
Besides, I want a moment with your daughter.

FRANCALOU

Lucille? Good, good. Then I'll attend the slaughter,
The *play*, with Pirandello on my arm—
See if this romp contains sufficient charm
To clear his mind of woes his kin beget.

LISETTE/LUCILLE

Have fun, then, "*Daddy*."

FRANCALOU
Yes, good night, Lisette.

(FRANCALOU EXITS.)

DAMIS
Lucille...Did he call you "Lisette"?

LISETTE/LUCILLE
Pet name.

DAMIS
Lisette or Meriadec, it's all the same.
For now I see, no matter how I feel,
That you were born to make another kneel,
That I'm not steel, but a genteel shlemiel,
That I must check, for good, my heartfelt zeal,
That I can't seek to suck on love's pastille.
In short, we're wrong no matter how I want.

LISETTE/LUCILLE
Who's right for me, then? Bouillabaisse?

DAMIS
Dorante.

(DORANTE ENTERS unnoticed and listens in. LISETTE has her back to him.)

LISETTE/LUCILLE
(strokes Damis's cheek)
Sweet man.

DAMIS
He's watching. Wishing for a kiss.

LISETTE/LUCILLE
Let's seal our separation, then—with this.

(She kisses DAMIS. We hear TINKLING STARS. DAMIS EXITS in a daze. LISETTE remains with her back to DORANTE until noted.)

DORANTE
Madame, don't let me interrupt your bliss.

LISETTE/LUCILLE
Dorante...

DORANTE
No, no, don't speak. All right, then, speak.
Explain how we could wander cheek to cheek

In this same wood not half a day ago—
How you could say "I love you," cheeks aglow,
How everything we had could so diminish.

(LUCILLE ENTERS and listens, standing right behind DORANTE, unnoticed.)

LISETTE/LUCILLE
Dorante...

DORANTE
Don't speak. Or speak. No, let me finish.
I only want to say—you are divine!
(LISETTE is trying to stifle a laugh as he gets more dramatic.)
You're trembling! But for whom? Who cares? You're mine!
You've been mine since before the birth of Jove!
Eons before we kissed within this grove.
You hate me?

LISETTE/LUCILLE
No.

DORANTE
You mean that kiss was real?!
You love me?

LISETTE/LUCILLE
Yes.

DORANTE
I *knew*! [*Kisses LISETTE.*]

LUCILLE
Dorante.

DORANTE
Lucille...

(Realizes:)
Lucille? Lucille! Lisette? Lisette!

LUCILLE
Lucille.

DORANTE
Lucille, I swear, this isn't what you think!

LISETTE/LUCILLE
Oh, sir, you're such a card. Wink, wink.

DORANTE
"*Wink, wink*"?!
Lisette—I mean, Lucille, I thought her you!

LUCILLE
She's dressing as me now. That's something new.
I think I spy a kink, for pink, so be my guest.

DORANTE
Lisette, will you please lay her fears to rest?

LISETTE/LUCILLE
Who, me?

DORANTE
How you're just costumed for a part?

LISETTE/LUCILLE
What part?

DORANTE
How I MISTOOK you, for a start?

LISETTE/LUCILLE
So you don't love me? That was all delusion? [*"Weeps."*]

DORANTE
(to LUCILLE)
She's joking! *Please!* Imagine my confusion!
Who *wouldn't* think her you in silhouette?

(MONDOR ENTERS, drunk and disheveled, carrying a BOTTLE.)

MONDOR
How's everybody doin'?—Hello, Lisette.
Oh, man, oh, man, am I a happy squirt?
You don't believe me, just check out my shirt.
Filet mignon, profiterole, some lipstick...
In the machine of life, I'm Cupid's dipstick!

(MONDOR dozes off standing up, leaning against LUCILLE.)

DORANTE
Don't tell me you're with this.

LUCILLE
I know he's stained.

DORANTE
You can't be serious.

The Metromaniacs   81

LUCILLE
I know you're pained.
Granted, he seems uncouth, to some degree.

DORANTE
He's Bozo!

LUCILLE
Yes. But *underneath*—Damis.

DORANTE
He's *not* Damis! And she, I thought, was you!

LISETTE
Miss Lucy, everything he says is true.
What can I do to show there's no foul play?

LUCILLE
Would you mind hosing down my fiancé?
And rendering him a bit less comatose?

LISETTE
He's kinda cute, if you look really close.

DORANTE
Well, thanks a lot, Lisette, for all your aid.

LISETTE
I'll just say this, monsieur: you're justly paid.
Mistrusting me, who's labored for your side?
I wouldn't tell you this but for this bride—
De Cosmos wrote a letter to your Dad.

DORANTE
Oh, God. Oh, no.

LISETTE
If you think *this* is bad...

DORANTE
If he hears that I'm here, I'll get the hook.

MONDOR
(waking up)
Is there more caviar?

LISETTE
Let's take a look.

(LISETTE and MONDOR EXIT.)

DORANTE
You heard her. *Well*, Lucille? I'm innocent!

LUCILLE
Oh, God, I wish I still were indolent.
But when Lisette brought me this lilting stanza [*produces POEM*]
I came to life...Life! That extravaganza
Where wife's not just a word nor love mere ink,
Where two lips warmly touch and, touching, drink.
With this I learned existence does exist,
From you I learned it's here, it's flesh, it's grist,
That skies are truly blue, birds really sing...
Except *you never WROTE the goddamn thing!*

DORANTE
I needed bait to win you, that came free!

LUCILLE
Who wrote it for you? Bouillabaisse?

DORANTE
                        Damis.

LUCILLE
Now wait a sec. Who's he...?

DORANTE
                        De Cosmos.

LUCILLE
                        Oh.
So now I have to marry *him?* Oh, no!

(*BALIVEAU ENTERS and listens from the "wood," unnoticed.*)

DORANTE
You're going to marry *me!* Except you can't.

LUCILLE
Not even if I want? Who's this "Dorante"?

DORANTE
Dorante. That's me.

LUCILLE
           Oh, God.

DORANTE
                        I'm incognodo.

LUCILLE

Nito.

DORANTE

You see? I told you I'm a dodo!

LUCILLE

Who cares? I love you! Now—why can't we wed?

DORANTE

Some legal case. Our Dads would have our head!

LUCILLE

And that's your ace? For that you'd give up hpe?
Well then to hell with parents! Let's elope.

DORANTE

We can't just...

LUCILLE

What's the problem, man? Be bold!

DORANTE

Your father...

LUCILLE

Oh, where are the knights of old?
I'll talk to Daddy. Legal case—avaunt!

(LUCILLE EXITS.)

DORANTE

But Lucy—hey, remember? Nonchalant?

(BALIVEAU steps forward.)

BALIVEAU

Monsieur, you are the son of old Geronte?

DORANTE

I am. Or was. I think. My brain's a turd.

BALIVEAU

It just so happens that I overheard.
Sir, I can help you in your amorous plight.
I know your fathers are estranged by spite
Yet I've the means to mend their ancient grudge.

DORANTE

But how? This law suit...

BALIVEAU
Young man, I'm a *judge*.
Abracadabra, I take on the case—
And each side wins with neither losing face.

DORANTE
I can't believe...! You'd really do all that?!

BALIVEAU
With pleasure—though there is a tit for tat. [*Shows FLYER.*]

DORANTE
Bouillabaisse!

BALIVEAU
Your foe, judging by your frown.
Well, I would like to see this play go *down*,
I want it booed until the last act ends.

DORANTE
It's done, monsieur. I can alert some friends.
We'll see to it the players are never heard.

BALIVEAU
A failure's guaranteed?

DORANTE
You have my word.

(DORANTE EXITS.)

BALIVEAU
(to us)
Alas, Damis's first play will be his last.

(BALIVEAU EXITS as DAMIS ENTERS. During this speech, the scene changes to evening around him. SERVANTS light lamps where noted.)

DAMIS
They should be starting soon. [*Checks watch.*]
This could be fast...
Maybe I'll sit. [*Sits.*] Or not. [*Stands up.*] Four minutes past.
The house is packed now, stacked up to the rings,
I see it all as though I'm in the wings—
Eye to the peephole. Yes, the dames and dandies
Have got their Playbills, bought their drinks and candies.
Upstairs, a mass of maids and one lone page.
Now one by one the lamps are lit onstage—
And at a stroke I doubt my every word.
My cast seems talent-free, my play absurd.
Here comes our lead. Applaud and look relaxed.

Oh, God, our ingénue—who should be axed...
Darling! Yes, break a leg! Mwah! Hold for laughter!
We changed that line, remember! See you after!
That actress is a penance for my sins.
Abruptly—curtain up! The play begins.
The crowd's gone quiet. What is this, mass hypnosis?
Oh, great. A cougher. Mass tuberculosis!
Was that a chuckle—somewhere at the back...?
Our ingenue's of course a *painted plaque*.
Speed up, speed up! Well, good. A solid laugh.
What are you...? *Speak!* Don't moo like some lost calf!
She flubbed her line. Show's over! That'll spoil it!
I'm in the men's room puking at a toilet.
Why didn't I trust my Uncle Baliveau?
He's wise, he's decent, generous, he should know...
Was that a laugh out there? Was that a *roar?*
Back to the peephole, watching someone—snore.
Some blimp who's barred my way to being famous.
The word is BUT, not AND, you ignoramus!
That was a hearty laugh. I may's well stay.
You know it's really not too bad, this play?
Thank God we hired that ingénue. She's brilliant!
I love these actors! Funny, smart, resilient.
But wait. Is that the final scene they're in...?
My guts have turned to sponge, my legs are tin.
Another laugh...another...now a burst!
The crowd's so wild you'd think they'd been rehearsed,
My lines are landing now like shining spears,
A line, a laugh, the final speech, and...cheers!
Shouts, rocking the Française! The crowd's ecstatic!
Someone is kissing me! Is this dramatic?
"Author" they're shouting. Is my collar straight?
I stride onstage and bow—Damis The Great!

(FRANCALOU and BALIVEAU ENTER.)

FRANCALOU

You missed it!

DAMIS

And your verdict Were you wowed?

FRANCALOU

You never saw a more illustrious crowd.
The King with Lady X., his current prop.

DAMIS

I mean, how went the *play*?

FRANCALOU

The play? A flop.

DAMIS
When you say "flop"...

BALIVEAU
Let's say no one was cooing.
You couldn't hear the lines through all the booing.

DAMIS
So—a catastrophe.

BALIVEAU
Par excellence.

DAMIS
But did it merit that malign response?

FRANCALOU
Well, I saw gleams of genius here and there,
Heard passages of wit and heart so rare
That words and thoughts conjoined like lovers kissing.

BALIVEAU
One hopes the author didn't hear the hissing.

DAMIS
Yet should he take to heart such passing shocks?
A pilot learns his trade amongst the rocks,
Not in the easy calm of balmy seas.
A tempest teaches better than a breeze.

FRANCALOU
Excelsior! Bravó, lad! That's the stuff!

DAMIS
Why should this playwright stop and cry "enough"
If this disaster makes his writing sager?

BALIVEAU
(pointedly, to DAMIS)
Unless this playwright's made a certain *wager*...?

FRANCALOU
(giving DAMIS a SEALED NOTE)
Oh, by the way, this letter came, express.

DAMIS
A note for me...? [*Reads it.*] Yes! Now things coalesce!

(DAMIS EXITS.)

FRANCALOU
Is he a wonder? I am such a fan.

BALIVEAU
You share his hobby.

FRANCALOU
No, I love the *man*!
His heart, his words! That pilot and those rocks?
Did you not hear? The pulse, the paradox?
If *he* wrote plays, all Paris would exult!
And I'd dare you to jeer at the result.

BALIVEAU
Get me my warrant. Then you'll see me thrilled.

FRANCALOU
I think your wish may just have been fulfilled.

BALIVEAU
How so?

FRANCALOU
I think he had it in his hand.

BALIVEAU
Who did?

FRANCALOU
De Cosmos.

BALIVEAU
I don't understand...

FRANCALOU
I told him of your nephew. He stepped in—
With such dispatch you'd think you two were kin.

BALIVEAU
God damn it all to hell!

FRANCALOU
What's all this pique?

BALIVEAU
Your protégé's the nephew whom I seek!

FRANCALOU
De Cosmos is Damis?

BALIVEAU
That's what I mean!

FRANCALOU
Good Lord! Then why this bitterness, this spleen?
He's upright, spirited, committed, true...

BALIVEAU
What you mean is that he's a fool like you!

FRANCALOU
You'd doom that gorgeous butterfly to Law?
How petty, how pathetic, how bourgeois!

BALIVEAU
I'll sue you, too! I'll put you in the pillory!
But what's this here? [*Finds PISTOLS.*] Some small artillery.
Take one. And he who's wrong is he who drops!

FRANCALOU
Baliveau...

BALIVEAU
Take it, blast you!

FRANCALOU
Those are props.

BALIVEAU
Then have him! I abandon him to you!

FRANCALOU
My friend, this is no way to say adieu.
So how's this for a plan to cure your angst?
He'll have my Lucy—and a million francs?
He mentioned that they'd had a passing fling.
The prelude to church chimes, that passing *ping*?
It's up to her, of course, or else it's deadlock.
But I've no doubt our clans were meant for wedlock.

BALIVEAU
A million francs...? And you thought that I was miffed!
I always knew he had a mighty gift.

FRANCALOU
I thought you'd see the light. My Baliveau!
(The two embrace. Calls:)
Monsieur Damis!

BALIVEAU
Who's he?

FRANCALOU
Your nephew.

BALIVEAU
Oh.

(DAMIS ENTERS.)

BALIVEAU
Ah, there you are! Congratulations, lad!

(BALIVEAU embraces him and dances about.)

DAMIS
I see since our last meeting you've gone mad.

BALIVEAU
Insane with glee, since how's this for a scheme?
You'll be his son-in-law! Is that a dream?

DAMIS
Lucille's a miracle. A jeweled cup.

BALIVEAU
See there? A perfect match!

DAMIS
We just broke up.

BALIVEAU
Broke UP?! Well, is there hope you'll...?

DAMIS
Not a speck.
I've lost Lucille, and with her...Meriadec.

FRANCALOU
Meriadec?

DAMIS
Meriadec. Who's Lucy 2.
(FRANCALOU lets out a hoot.)
Why are you laughing, sir?

FRANCALOU
Oh, not at you
But at the genius of our jokester gods.

Whose plots defy all dramaturgic odds.
Lucy and Meriadec! You thought her she?

DAMIS
You mean she's not? So Meriadec's still free?

BALIVEAU
What in God's name are you two ON about?!

DAMIS
Here comes Lucille right now, to quash all doubt.

(LISETTE ENTERS, dressed as herself again.)

DAMIS
Lucille...But why're you dressed as a soubrette?

LISETTE
A what?

DAMIS
A maid.

LISETTE
I'm sorry, have we met?

FRANCALOU
Cosmo, may I present our maid, Lisette.

BALIVEAU
Who this girl is, is unassailable!
The point is, *Lucy's* still available!

DAMIS
What about Meriadec?

BALIVEAU
Will you forget her?

DAMIS
How can I uncle, when I've never met her?

BALIVEAU
You've met Lucille, though?

DAMIS
Frankly, I don't know.
I do know here's Lucille's most recent beau.

(MONDOR ENTERS, out of the fancy livery, hung over.)

MONDOR
Nobody talk. My brain is oozing booze.

BALIVEAU
This lout?!

MONDOR
The grumpy uncle from Toulouse!

FRANCALOU
Fess up! Who are you in this maddening maze?

MONDOR
To tell the truth, it's all a kind of haze.
My costume's off, so I'm myself, I seem...
Oh, I have had the most amazing dream!
Words cannot hear! Eyes cannot see! And so on.
I was in love, by what I have to go on.
This cuckoo girl in a luxurious house.
The joint looked just like this...

BALIVEAU
(takes him by the collar)
Excuse me—*louse*.

MONDOR
Monsieur, you have my absolute attention.

BALIVEAU
Are you Lucille's, too or is that invention?

MONDOR
It's kind of hard to tell with all the wine

LISETTE
Forget the wine, forget Lucille, you're mine.

MONDOR
I knew you looked familiar!
(Bends LISETTE over in a big kiss.)
Yeah, it's her!

BALIVEAU
Will you stop that?

MONDOR
What's it to you, monsieur?
We're poor folk but we're horny. Find your own!

FRANCALOU
Here comes the real Lucille.

LISETTE
Or Lucy's clone.

(LUCILLE ENTERS.)

FRANCALOU
Sweetheart—you *are* my daughter, I assume—
Behold the man I'd like to be your groom.
A blazing nova yet to glow at peak.

LUCILLE
Excuse me, father, but if I might speak?

LUCILLE
You see, there's one small problem, and here's why:
I am in *luvvvvv*. Oh, God, I want the guy!
I see that dimple where his lower lips joins?
I get this smoldering deep down in my *loins*,
I want us groin-to-groin from dawn to dusk,
I want to smell his stink, I crave his musk.
I want him now and I want him *forever*.

FRANCALOU
Well, quite a change from Mademoiselle Whatever!
He's literary, too—your fragrant friend?

LUCILLE
I doubt he's read a sentence end to end.
But who would judge a man by any book
Who broadcasts poetry with his every look?

FRANCALOU
Then there's no problem! Or am I deluded?
But wait, is this the fellow I excluded?
I had good evidence...

LUCILLE
You've lost your plea.
You thought he had a girlfriend? She was me!

FRANCALOU
Then I exclude him now because his father
Has caused me years of dreary legal bother.

BALIVEAU
May we return to our end of the plot?
Will your Lucille betroth Damis or not?

DAMIS
I am Damis.

ALL
We know!

BALIVEAU
A genius, lass,
If in his previous life a rampant ass.

(DORANTE ENTERS.)

DORANTE
All right, so have I won? I'm hers to choose?

BALIVEAU
Excuse me, but I'm leaving for Toulouse.

DORANTE
Now just a minute here. We had a pact!
You'd back me if I got this play attacked.
(Shows FLYER, and points to MONDOR.)
A play by *him*, no less! Who's gotten his due!

MONDOR
Not quite. You missed an episode or two.
(Moves Dorante's pointing finger to indicate DAMIS.)

DORANTE
You wrote this play?

DAMIS
I was the perpetrator.

DORANTE
Well, this whole mix-up has your imprimatur.
Revenge, for tangling Lucy in your net!

DAMIS
In this case I think Lucy was Lisette.

FRANCALOU
Enough! I don't care who, what, where or why!
Lucy will never, not while I stand by,
Marry the son of my old nemesis!
I swear it!

DAMIS
Sir, you might just glance at this. [*Gives LETTER.*]
It's from his father and may change your mind.

FRANCALOU
I've sworn an oath no letter can unbind—
(Glances at LETTER. Thunderstruck:)
Good *God!* Why, it's a full and fond retraction!
Professing love—regretting all detraction—
Signed here "Geronte" with his familiar cramp.
Though tears have softened it. See there, it's *damp!*
(Joining the hands of DORANTE and LUCILLE.)
I now pronounce you man and wife. We're done.

DORANTE
But sir, your oath...

FRANCALOU
You're married lad. Have fun.

ALL
HOORAY!

DORANTE
Wait, wait! Before we two can blend
I have to beg forgiveness from my friend.
I scotched his play, misread him to a fault...

DAMIS
Oh, let's not spoil this feast with excess salt.
My matrimoniac friend, you have my *thanks*.
For what a day! From facing death by blanks
To falling deep in love and getting slapped—
I'm still not sure by whom, but that seems apt—
These hours were packed with life, real life, galore.
So thank you, sir—you two—Lisette—Mondor,
For such demented, transcendental woe.
Plus extra-special thanks to Baliveau!

LISETTE & LUCILLE & DORANTE
Who's Baliveau?

DAMIS
Kid bro' to my begetter.

LISETTE
Well, if you're Baliveau I have a letter...
[Gives BALIVEAU a LETTER.]

BALIVEAU
This? This is from my ex-wife in Peru!

MONDOR
(I see our exposition isn't through.)

BALIVEAU
"*Have spent so many nights here missing you.*
And just discovered veins of silver ore.
Would we could locate our lost son Mondor."

MONDOR & DAMIS & LISETTE
MONDOR!

DORANTE
Now wait! Who's he?

MONDOR
Mondor? That's *me!*

[*Grabs LETTER.*]

BALIVEAU
(*embracing MONDOR*)
M'ijo!

MONDOR
Mi padre!

LISETTE
How'd that letter *reach* you?!

MONDOR
Who cares? We own a mine in Machu Picchu!

LUCILLE
But poor Damis is left with none to dote on.

DAMIS
For that you'd have to find my lost Bretonne,
Mysterious Meriadec de Peauduncqville!
God knows if my mad muse was ever real.
Her memory will always harry me.

FRANCALOU
Then there's just one solution. [*Kneels.*] *Marry me!*

DAMIS
You're *she*?

FRANCALOU
As surely as you are Damis.

DAMIS
Yes, but. Yes, but. Yes, but...

FRANCALOU
But?

DAMIS
Oh, all right.

FRANCALOU
Who would have dreamed this was my wedding night?

BALIVEAU
If this is drama, I am truly smote!
In fact, I'd like to read a play I wrote…

MONDOR
Let's save that, Dad—till dinner's in our hand.

DORANTE
There's one plot point I still don't understand…
[THEY ALL shout him down.]

FRANCALOU
My friends, we've food and drink to sate five score.
Let's feast until it's gone, then feast some more!
And there's a sylvan grove in this salon
Where those in love may wander till it's dawn.
Do as you please! Enjoy! That's all I ask!
(To audience)
And with that blessing I may now—unmask.
You see, this day once happened. It's all true—
Except for this: I wasn't Francalou.
Oh, he was there, his house, a painted tree.
He was my host, and my name was…Damis.
These hours of lunacy sparked my career,
Started me writing plays like this one here,
And taught me life's a multi-stranded plot
So intricate who knows who tied each knot!
Too mad, you say? Too many a twisted switch?
It's how my plays are made—and why I'm rich.
I wish you all such madness, as your friend,
And may your exposition never, ever end!

CURTAIN

END OF PLAY